PRAISE FOR *GRACIOUS UNCERTAINTY*

"Jane Sigloh's *Gracious Uncertainty* seems like a sure bet to me. She has the wisdom that comes (if lucky) 'at a certain age,' but a youthful spirit that doesn't settle for received wisdom or a stock response. She investigates experience across her own lifetime to share both what she has come to understand and what remains a mystery. The Bible is her companion throughout but by no means her only inspiration. Best of all, she makes you want to keep better track of yourself. God may be beyond knowing, but what are the hints and guesses that come to us if, like her, we pay attention to our lives?" **—Peter S. Hawkins, Yale Divinity School**

"Jane Sigloh validates the statement, 'God made human beings, because he loves stories.' Her stories and reflections are personal but, as Carl Rogers says, 'that which is most personal is most universal.' Jane's memories and reflections are woven into a practical theology, and they are a sound basis to finding a footing in life's second half." **—J. Pittman McGehee, Episcopal priest, Jungian analyst, and author of *The Invisible Church: Finding Faith Where You Are***

GRACIOUS UNCERTAINTY
Faith in the Second Half of Life

JANE SIGLOH

ROWMAN & LITTLEFIELD
Lanham • Boulder • New York • London

Biblical quotes come from various bibles.

Published by Rowman & Littlefield
A wholly owned subsidiary of The Rowman & Littlefield Publishing Group, Inc.
4501 Forbes Boulevard, Suite 200, Lanham, Maryland 20706
www.rowman.com

Unit A, Whitacre Mews, 26-34 Stannary Street, London SE11 4AB, United Kingdom

Distributed by NATIONAL BOOK NETWORK

British Library Cataloguing in Publication Information available

Library of Congress Cataloging-in-Publication Data available
Names: Sigloh, Jane, 1934– author.
Title: Gracious uncertainty : faith in the second half of life / Jane Sigloh.
Description: Lanham : Rowman & Littlefield, 2017. | Includes bibliographical references.
Identifiers: LCCN 2017031631 (print) | LCCN 2017033056 (ebook) | ISBN 9781442276260 (electronic) | ISBN 9781442276253 (pbk. : alk. paper)
Subjects: LCSH: Older Christians—Religious life. | Aging—Religious aspects—Christianity.
Classification: LCC BV4580 (ebook) | LCC BV4580 .S539 2017 (print) | DDC 248.8/5—dc23
LC record available at https://lccn.loc.gov/2017031631

∞™ The paper used in this publication meets the minimum requirements of American National Standard for Information Sciences—Permanence of Paper for Printed Library Materials, ANSI/NISO Z39.48-1992.

For
Ethan MacNeill Engleby
1960–2008

Go now; write it before them on a tablet, and inscribe it in a book, so that it may be for the time to come as a witness forever.

—ISAIAH 30:8

Contents

Contents

FOREWORD
Julie Shields and James Lott

ABOUT THE TIME WE REALIZE THAT WE ARE MORTAL—WHICH is frequently quite a while after we realize that other people are mortal—many of us start fretting about what we want to leave behind. Who will inherit my grandmother's quilt? Who will get the grandfather clock? And that crystal vase that's been in the family forever?

But we also want to leave behind a part of ourselves.

One way is to leave our stories, so our children and grandchildren will know about us and the world we live in. This is partly what Jane Sigloh is doing in this collection. The stories, told with skill and grace and wisdom, are a special gift to her readers. With her eye for details, she creates scenes that come to life before us. We picture a young Jane sitting in church with her grandmother on a scorching Texas Sunday morning, or an older Jane, having fallen while taking a supper upstairs, sitting in the middle of avocados and grapefruit and dirt and dog hair. We feel the insensitivity and ignorance of her grandchild Henry's teacher, and we laugh at the sight of Jane holding on to her nineteen inch fish as she falls overboard and heads downstream.

But as good as Jane's stories are and as much as we get to know her and her world, this is far more than a collection of funny and touching stories forming a memoir. The stories summon meditations on what is most important to her: her faith. It is that faith she wants to share, the faith that has sustained her, given her joy, and borne her through sorrow. And with which she lovingly—always lovingly—struggles.

Jane takes her spiritual experiences seriously but takes herself lightly; a happy blend. Not like a wild-eyed evangelist on a street corner grabbing your arm, nor like a scholarly professor at a seminary occasionally lapsing into Greek (though she has the passion of the one and the erudition of the other); she greets us as a friend sharing her stories and the thoughts that arise from them.

Like a good friend, she shares intimate moments of her life— the loss of those she loves, times of helplessness and exhaustion, moments of wonder and joy. And especially, what may be hardest for any of us to share, moments of questioning and doubt. These are not academic reflections, nor are they sermons. They are personal, sometimes quirky, always honest inquiries into life's puzzles and quandaries. As a whole they probe the meaning of God's providence in our lives.

Typically, each reflection begins with a memory (or sometimes with a casual observation) and the memory or the observation generates a search for insight. As our guide in the search, Jane is sometimes amusing, often herself bemused, but ultimately the conveyor of an essential wisdom.

For many, aging can result in calcified certainties, in despair over loss, or in a nostalgia that is ultimately delusive. But these reflections provide a different model of the wisdom that can come to us as we grow older: the capacity to wonder about life, to open ourselves to the wind of the Spirit, and to rest in what Jane calls "gracious uncertainty." As thinking and faithful people, this collection tells us, we can achieve in age an ability to accept our limited capacity to comprehend God's mystery while at the same time glorying in God's love.

This collection will speak to those who are living with the challenges of aging and to those who love and counsel them: pastors, families, and friends. But the reflections are also relevant to anyone, young or old or somewhere in between, concerned with spiritual questions, not because the reflections provide answers—certainly not dogmatic answers—but because they show how to go about asking those questions with faith *and* with honesty.

One final—and personal—note: a blurb on the cover of Jane's previous book *Like Trees Walking* described her as "a priest, wife, mother, grandmother, teacher, poet, vintner, cook, gardener, and story keeper." We'd like to add "friend." We have both known Jane for years and have been on the receiving end of her affection, humor, and wisdom. We believe readers of this collection will receive the same.

Years ago, one of us—Julie—attended a Bible study that Jane was teaching. Julie didn't know Jane well then and was a bit intimidated. When Jane turned to her and asked a question, Julie, surrounded by those who had been studying the Bible for months and whom she assumed knew far more than she, confessed, "Most of my theology comes from Shakespeare." Without batting an eye, Jane responded, "Well, the Gospel is still being written." And so it is.

Acknowledgments

I want to acknowledge with gratitude the many friends who supported this work from its conception to its publication. Jim Lott guided me through pivotal themes in the manuscript, reading draft after draft after draft. He understood what I was trying to say and offered suggestions with clarity and a deep respect for the discipline of writing as an instrument of faith.

Julie Shields read every chapter with a critical eye and a poet's imagination. Her candor with regard to theology prompted me to reconsider the paradoxical source of truth. She also made me laugh whenever I tried to make sense out of the senseless.

Thanks to Fred L. Horton, professor emeritus of Wake Forest University, who provided valuable insights into the meaning of forgiveness. To Jemile Safaraliyeva, who devoted countless hours and careful attention to the bibliography. And to the editors at Rowman & Littlefield who offered judicial advice with regard to technicalities, organization, and the sequence of chapters.

Most important, I want to thank my beloved husband, Denny. He was the inspiration for a *gracious uncertainty* in the journey of *his* faith. And while he often wondered if I would ever finish this book, he patiently endured my propensity to labor over the minute details of a paragraph. He also encouraged me with steadfast assurance that I was doing what I was supposed to be doing.

I owe a debt of gratitude to my children as well because their lives . . . full of adventure and thoughtful enterprise mixed with heartbreaking losses . . . were a rich resource for stories (some of which are accurately rendered).

To others, unnamed but remembered, I give my thanks. This book is your gift to readers.

Chapter 1

Sand Castles

IF YOU LIVE NEAR THE BEACH, YOU LEARN HOW TO MAKE SAND castles. Starting where the sand is packed and solid, you build a foundation wide enough to sustain a few towers. Then come turrets molded in cups of pressed sand. And if you're careful, you can carve steps going all the way to the top of the turrets. That's where you put a flag that says, "This is *my* tower." Finally there's the moat. You have to have a moat to protect the castle from invaders. And a bridge to let armored knights back into its stronghold.

Sand castles can be quite magnificent.

But they don't last. Children in the mood for mischief leap up and land on top of their walls, mocking their stability. And there's always the wind that blows steadily across the surface of the beach until all that's left is an unidentified lump of sand. And the white, washed waves pull it back into the sea.

I think sand castles are a lot like the Kingdom that the Lord appointed Jeremiah to "pull down, destroy, and overthrow."[1] And I think they're a lot like the kingdom of our faith. We build towers and turrets housing firm convictions about love, prayer, scripture, sin, judgment, salvation, and so on. We dig a moat around them so we can defend the walls from others who mock their stability.

Eventually, in the grace of time, we start to watch the wind soften the outline of our convictions. That's a good thing. And it's a good thing for the waves to wash a few of them out to sea. But sometimes . . . tragically . . . a cold blast of bad weather topples the towers. Pummels them with rain. And we walk away, abandoning the castle altogether.

Yet often in our older age the Spirit endows us with wisdom. And we remember that the Lord also appointed Jeremiah to "build and to plant." So that's what we do . . . with God's help. We build and plant. Pulling the foundation of our castle back up to the edge of the beach. Making towers and turrets out of experience. Even though they're a bit wobbly, they're still tall . . . much taller than they were before. (We leave out the moat, hoping others will join a conversation in the Great Hall.) And by the time we've settled into the stillness of age, we're ready to listen for the wind. Watch it settle the sand over our convictions and stir them once again.

That's what this book is about. Sand castles.

CHAPTER 2

Where the Wind Blows

WHEN MY MOTHER WAS IN HER EIGHTIES, SHE STARTED PUTTING things in little plastic bags . . . bracelets, candies, beads, everything. She even put plastic bags in plastic bags and fastened them with a rubber band. I guess it gave her a sense of security. So much is uncertain when you're eighty years old. Seeing, hearing, walking. Where am I going? How do I know the way?

And today the world seems bent on making it even more uncertain . . . with things like modems and routers and clouds . . . techie clouds that contain a gazillion gigabytes of information. It's enough to make you buy lots of plastic bags so you can at least pretend you're in control.

Lately I've discovered that uncertainty isn't restricted to eighty-year-olds. Or seventy-year-olds. Indeed, contrary to what scientists used to say, uncertainty seems to be the law of the universe. They used to say that the natural world is an inerrant machine. We could discover its workings by applying the law of cause and effect. "*This* is so because *that* is so." And even if science didn't know everything, it assumed it would know it eventually.

But then Einstein discovered that light didn't travel according to the laws of the universe. It seemed to have a mind of its own, bending and warping with time and space. So what had been quite orderly and predictable became "relative." Physicists said "*This* is so because . . . *well, it depends.*"

And quantum physicists discovered that the atom, long considered the basic building block of matter, really wasn't basic after all. There was something inside it . . . a nucleus of protons and neutrons surrounded by a swarm of orbiting electrons. And there were still smaller particles inside the nucleus . . . quarks, neutrinos, and muons.

I sent a text message to my grandson asking him what it all meant and he responded: "*bndles enrg.*" Oh good, that clarifies everything.

But according to my grandson's exceedingly patient message, if you travel down as far as you can through the subatomic chain, you reach (according to the theory) a tiny one-dimensional loop they call a string. The string is like a thin piece of elastic that jiggles with a strange erratic grace.

And the thing that makes up the thing that makes up the string . . . is a bundle of energy (*bndles enrg*). It's a wild and crazy bundle that can enter other dimensions and roam through the fabric of the universe in a trillionth of a trillionth of a second. It can even disappear completely and reappear in another place without traveling the distance in between. Which is why my mother put bracelets, candies, and beads in little plastic bags and fastened them with a rubber band.

Not that she knew anything about quantum physics. She never thought about the variable path of light from the moon to the terrace or the thing that makes up the thing that makes up the string. And she totally trusted Newton's law of cause and effect. "*This* is so because *that* is so." And if you erred and strayed like lost sheep, *that* would be so.

But as the years followed years, life changed. Things seemed to disappear completely and reappear in another place without traveling the distance in between. "Where did I put my glasses?" What had once been quite orderly and predictable became relative. Then the children moved away. The postman died. The roof leaked. And the Red Sox lost the pennant. It was enough to make anyone put things in little plastic bags. If only to create the illusion of order and certainty.

The big question, however, is why have *I* started to do the same thing? Our children have moved away, but I can still see their faces in plastic picture frames. And I have grandchildren who send me text messages. But somehow things aren't the way they used to be. Half of the time I don't understand what people are saying. They're like a swarm of orbiting electrons. I wake up in the middle of the night and watch the luminous dial of the clock move toward 5:00 a.m All of which is compounded by a vague disquietude. I do not know the way. I do not know the measure of my days.

Sometimes I wish I were a fundamentalist. Fundamentalists are such faithful experts of the unknowable. But I'm not a fundamentalist. I'm a second generation bag lady who doesn't know the why or where or how or when of ultimate questions in life. And every time I throw the questions out into the deep, I can hear God's voice . . . stern with reprimand. "Where were you when I laid the foundation of the earth and prescribed boundaries for the sea. Where were you when I said, 'thus far shall you come, and no farther, and here shall your proud waves be stopped.'"[1]

And so I stop. Reluctantly. All I can do is stand at the boundaries of the sea.

But at least I'm in good company. Modern physicists have conceded that the grand certainties of classical science are gone. All they have now are elusive theories about black holes and bundles of energy. You can't put those in plastic bags and fasten them with a rubber band. And in their negative capacity they know that there are unknown unknowns that they don't know they don't know.

I'm also in the good company of mystics. But what's different . . . what's *saintly* . . . is that instead of pounding their fists against the boundaries, the great mystics seemed to be at home with their unknowing. "The wind blows where it chooses, and you hear the sound of it, but you do not know where it comes from or where it goes."[2]

Imagine such gracious uncertainty.

I'm going to try to cultivate it and accept the fact that I do not know how *bndles enrg* enter other dimensions and roam through the curled fabric of the universe. Or why . . . in spite of all those bright and happy hymns . . . life is not as well ordered as we would like for it to be. I'm going to try and listen for the sound of the wind and follow its currents through the mountain peaks without concern for its direction.

And when my earthly life is gathered up in the sweep of time I'll stand alongside the scientists and mystics and proclaim with absolute certainty that even though I did not know the way, God did, and God brought a magnificent order and beauty to the universe.

All the way down the subatomic chain
    to a tiny one-dimensional loop
        called a *string*.

CHAPTER 3

Hearing and Listening

WHEN MY GRANDSON WAS IN HIS TERRIBLE TWOS (WHICH lasted for approximately eight years), he would cover his ears whenever he heard something he didn't want to hear . . . like, "Stop chasing the cat." He perfected his nonlistening skills with a recitative fortissimo "Lalalalalala."

But when he grew up (and he *did* grow up) he became a youthful elder, full of wisdom. I was at the computer one day when he walked into the room and asked a question. I said, "Yeah. I guess so." Which was basically a nonanswer.

He asked the question again. And again my answer was dismissive. "Oma," he said, "You're not listening."

"Yes, I am."

"No! You're hearing, but you're not listening."

Ouch!

Hearing and listening . . . they're not the same, are they? I have hearing aids and they're very useful when it comes to communication. (People don't speak up the way they used to.) But listening requires so much more attention. You have to pull away from your computer and cell phone. You have to abandon Facebook. And you have to ignore the temptation to interrupt the other's conversation with, "That reminds me of the time that I was in New York and . . ."

It's similar to the way people listened to each other on the Feast of Pentecost. The story in Acts is usually considered a miracle of the tongue. And indeed it was. "They were all together in one place when there came from the sky a noise like that of a driving wind. . . . And there appeared to them tongues as of fire resting on each of them. And they began to talk in other languages as the Spirit gave them power of utterance."[1]

But the more I think about it, the more I realize that Pentecost wasn't just a miracle of the tongue. It was a miracle of the ear. "They were amazed and wondered, saying, 'Are not all these who are speaking Galileans? And how is it that we hear, each of us in his own native language?'"[2] Parthians listened to the Medes and the Medes listened to the Phrygians and Elamites listened to . . . *somebody*.

Like the miracle of the tongue, it was a response of the Spirit . . . a noise like that of a driving wind. And it prompted the Parthians, the Medes, the Phrygians, and the Elamites to abandon the self-absorbing *me* and make room for the other in their space. It said, "I'm interested in what *you're* doing, where *you've* been, and how *your* grandchildren are growing out of their terrible twos."

It's the way of love, isn't it? Not preferential love. It doesn't have anything to do with *feelings* (except when it comes to my grandson). I'm not inclined to *hug* the woman down the street, the one with the yappy dog. But sometimes the Spirit prompts me to *listen* to her. Listen to what she's saying about a china pattern at the Belk store or how I should wait a month before I trim the lilac trees.

It's like the love that the Hasidic theologian Martin Buber talks about in *I and Thou* . . . an unsentimental substantial love of a subject for a subject as opposed to a subject for an object . . . an object of indifference.

The *I and Thou* kind of love puts us in a respectful relationship with everyone . . . from the stranger on the bus to the child who needs an honest answer. Listening isn't about communication. It's about communion.

Joseph Campbell tells the story of a day on his lecture tour in the San Francisco area. His hosts said the event would be held at a synagogue in Marin, and so to make sure he was on time he arrived a half hour early. Spotting the synagogue, he parked his car a short distance from the entrance and started walking away when a small boy, about six years old, said, "You can't park here."

Campbell glanced around and said, "Why can't I park here? There isn't a *No Parking* sign and no red stripe on the curb. So why can't I park here?"

"Because I'm a fire hydrant."

Campbell responded instantly. "Oh, thank you! I could have gotten a parking ticket!" With that he walked back to his car, unlocked it, and parked fifty feet away from the boy.[3]

How *loving* that was of Campbell! He didn't just *hear* the boy. He *listened* to him, treated him as a *thou*, and *responded* to the truth of his imagination.

I want to be like him. I want to listen to those who speak in other tongues and those who have no voice. I want to listen to neighbors with yappy dogs, to the woman who checks out my groceries, and the man who fixes our lawn mower.

I want to listen to fire hydrants.

CHAPTER 4

Yoke of Freedom

IF YOU GREW UP IN THE 1950S, FREEDOM WAS A RARE COMMODITY. We studied its civic value and dressed up as pilgrims on Thanksgiving in memory of those who sought it in America. But as for personal freedom, there was precious little of that. Peter Gomes referred to a "consortium of power,"[1] which included parents, teachers, preachers, nurses, librarians, and the sidewalk patrol, that ruled over us. It was usually a "benevolent tyranny," but we frequently had to serve time for things done and left undone.

When I was fifteen, my parents decided I would be better off in a place with more structure, so I was sent away to boarding school. There were lots of dos and don'ts and oughts and shoulds at that school. No one mentioned individual rights or entitlements. We studied, played vigorous sports (probably to keep our minds off the pleasures that kids outside our walls enjoyed), and went to chapel every day.

On Friday afternoons we were allowed to walk to town, escorted by a chaperone who saw to it that we didn't buy any contraband. Contraband in those days consisted of lipstick, chewing gum, and movie magazines.

When I tell young people about those days, they find it hard to believe. Surely I'm lifting scenes out of a nineteenth-century novel. But as Peter Gomes said, "I lived in such a place . . . and in an environment that to some . . . might seem stifling, uncreative, and even repressed, [but] I felt free to grow."[2]

But looking back at the 1950s, I remember how quickly the "benevolent tyranny" was toppled in a wave of protest that roared into the 1960s. People were swept away in the spirit of the age . . . no more chaperones and a lot more contraband. As Paul said in his letter to the Galatians: "For freedom, Christ has set us free. Stand firm, therefore, and do not submit to a yoke of slavery."[3]

Amen to that!

And yet . . . I guess it's my age or maybe the memory of all the boarding school dos and don'ts and oughts and shoulds . . . I've started to feel a hint of protest *against* freedom. I know that sounds crazy, but . . . have I misunderstood Paul's letter to the Galatians? Did Christ set us free for the sake of autonomy? Independence?

Last week someone told me that her husband was going to Florida on vacation. I thought that was a fairly liberal arrangement . . . giving each other occasional space. "How long will he be gone?"

"A month."

A month! Her husband was leaving her for a month! "What's he going to do?"

"Nothing much. Just hang out with his buddies."

No way! I wonder what I would do if *my* husband decided to go away for a month of fun in the sun? (It wouldn't be nice.) And just "hanging out"? Is that what freedom is all about? Leading a detached life with endless choices and no commitments?

I don't think that's what Paul was talking about in the letter to the Galatians. For him, life was never without obligations and commitments. The only question was whether he "belonged to Christ or belonged to sin." No hanging out in between. And his whole idea of freedom was based on the memory of God liberating Israel from the bondage of Egypt through which we became God's *possession*. "You are my people and I am your God." It was impossible to lead a detached life with endless choices and no commitments.

So I guess we aren't *that* free, are we? It's complicated. God liberates us ... giving us the right to choose ... and simultaneously binds us to him.

But maybe what Paul was talking about is more profoundly liberating than a detached life could ever be. Jesus says, "Take my yoke upon you and learn from me; for I am gentle and humble in heart. Here you will find rest for your souls. For my yoke is easy and my burden is light."[4]

It sounds like a *gentle* tyranny, doesn't it? I think I can submit to that. Even if the yoke scrapes my shoulders a bit, I'd be free. Free from the despair that often haunts us as we grow old. Free from all the wasted hours and days ... wandering around from pillar to post. With a gentle yoke I'd be free to do what I'm *supposed* to do. What I *want* to do. What I'm *called* to do. I could put things in their proper perspective and greet the true reason for living as God's *possession*.

I'd feel free to grow.

And, who knows, maybe I'd find rest for my soul.

CHAPTER 5

The Wonder of It All

IT'S AMAZING! LAST WEEK A NASA SPACECRAFT ABOUT THE size of a piano flew within 7,800 miles of Pluto. It was a close encounter and a great scientific accomplishment considering the fact that it traveled three billion miles.

Astronomers are hoping the spacecraft's "multispectral camera" and "infrared mapping spectrometer" will give them clues about the origin of the solar system. What numerical accidents conspired to make our planet habitable? If gravity were a fraction stronger or weaker we wouldn't be here.

And the little ship . . . called New Horizons . . . is still on the move . . . venturing into the vast region beyond Neptune called the Kuiper belt. Planets in that region are mostly chunks of ice, but they're like time capsules, frozen remnants of our early cosmic history.

Is there no limit to scientific discoveries?

Back in 1972 I saw a photograph of Earth taken from Apollo 17 (remember that blue and white swirling mass?) and I thought, "This is the ultimate. Scientists can go no further in the exploration of outer space."

But I was wrong. Limitations are more like invitations when it comes to astronomy. The Hubble telescope, launched in 1990, is still reflecting the marvels of the universe: undiscovered satellites, a fiery nebula shaped like a doughnut, huge towers of interstellar gas and dust. And just a few months ago scientists at Cape Canaveral identified a "close cousin to earth." Imagine that—a planet orbiting a sun-like star. And someone might even call it "my home." It's fascinating and a tribute to the genius of scientific minds.

But where is God in all this?

Skeptics say nowhere. Modern science has rendered the idea of a divine Creator obsolete. "The entire universe, matter, radiation and even space itself arose spontaneously out of nothing."[1]

Out of nothing? It's hard for me to get my head around "nothing." And the longer I live the more convinced I am that before there was anything there was a divine being who brought something out of nothing.

I can't explain why I believe that. It defies logical analysis and scientific proof. But as Karen Armstrong said in her book *The Case for God*, "Religion wasn't something tacked on to the human condition, an optional extra imposed by unscrupulous priests. The desire to cultivate a sense of the transcendent may be *the* defining human characteristic."[2]

And in the premodern era people believed that a deeper truth emerged when they let their imaginations flourish. So they didn't cultivate a sense of the transcendent with logical analysis (the recognized way of thinking when it came to practical matters). They cultivated it with ritual, music, dance, . . . and a story.

Once upon a time . . . as in Genesis.

The earth was without form and void. And God said, "A formless void will never do. We need dry land to separate it from the waters." And it was so. Then God said, "Now let's put a dome over the waters." And suddenly a dome rose up out of the waters . . . like a whale breeching the ocean waves. God called the dome "Sky."

But you could hardly see the Sky. So God made the two great lights. The greater light . . . a huge ball of fire . . . to rule the day.

And a lesser light . . . with a romantic luster . . . to rule the night. And as if that weren't enough, God swept his hand across the dome and millions of stars trailed off the end of his fingers.

God was very pleased . . . but also a little worried. With all the intersecting orbits in the dome, there could be traffic problems. So God set in place some natural laws so the lights could move around the Sky without bumping into each other or collapsing on themselves (except maybe now and then).

That's the cosmic part of the story. The biological part began 3.5 billion years ago. That's when God decided to make human beings out of the dust of the ground and give them the capacity to understand the natural laws that enable the lights to move around the Sky without bumping into each other or collapsing on themselves (except maybe now and then). And it was so.

Then God invited the human beings to shake off the dust of the ground and look up to the Sky. There . . . far above their reach was a curtain of beaded lace so bright it totally covered the darkness.

It's a good story. Of course, it's *not* good science. It doesn't pretend to be. It isn't interested in *how* God created his universe. It just tells *why* he did it. It says he prefers what *is* to what is *not,* and so he creates what *is* and gives us all the capacity to wonder, to gaze in awe at what he has done.

And I can still remember the time when the skies gave birth to a sense of wonder in me. I was a child, lying on a wooden dock that stretched out over Galveston Bay . . . listening to the water lap at the barnacled pilings. My father was trying to explain cosmology to my sister and me, but above us was a shoal of stars so amazing that I couldn't hear what he was saying. It was as if I could see the whole universe from where I was on that wooden dock.

"Look," I cried, pointing my finger at a shooting star in the second that it disappeared. And even as a child . . . or maybe because I was a child . . . I sensed that there was something beyond the stars. We see that same sensibility in the psalmist's words:

O Lord my God, how excellent is your greatness!
You are clothed with majesty and splendor.
You wrap yourself with light as with a cloak.
And spread out the heavens like a curtain.[3]

And I think it's the same sensibility that prompts scientists to build little spacecrafts the size of a piano and go on one adventure after another. (With every discovery you can hear the "bravos" echoing through the halls of heaven.) And their wonder isn't just about what they've discovered, it's about something beyond what they see with multispectral cameras and infrared mapping spectrometers . . . something transcendent, supreme, on another plane of reality. In a curious way their awakening to the majesty and splendor allows us to reconcile religion and science. They're not conflicting truths. They're complementary.

Who knows what else scientists will discover as they move out in time and space? People keep telling me, "watch your step." But how can I spend the end of my days watching my steps? There's no excitement in that . . . no awe or inspiration. I'd rather hold on to a strong arm and look up to the millions of stars
that are still trailing
off the end of God's fingers.

Chapter 6

Matter Matters

The name of the movie is *O Brother, Where Art Thou?* It's about three escaped convicts searching for a cache of money during the depression era. My favorite scene is one in which the character Delmar notices a man standing in the middle of a river baptizing a long line of white-robed candidates. Delmar decides to join them. He rushes into the river, gets dunked, and emerges with a triumphant cry, "I've been saved."

How good it is of God to create laughter.

But the scene reminded me of the time our grandson Keene was baptized. He wore my grandmother's christening gown (over the objections of his father who thought he should wear baby blue jeans). We fed him into somnolence, praying he wouldn't throw up on the gown. The minister poured a handful of water over his head in the name of the Father, the Son, and the Holy Spirit. Keene woke up immediately and smiled (which may or may not have been the equivalent of Delmar's triumphant cry).

Of course, in the early days of the church a handful of water wouldn't do. Candidates had to be *dunked* . . . just like Delmar . . . dunked three times so they could *feel* salvation . . . as in birthing, bathing, quenching, drowning, and breathlessly emerging from the deep.

Things changed, however. Over the years baptism was reduced to a single dunk, then to a quick splash from the font, and finally a sprinkling from a finger bowl. Who knows . . . it may eventually be reduced to a mist. But no matter how many changes were made, there was always water . . . that natural, tangible, visible element that brings the theological wind down to earth. I like that.

Maybe it's my aging weakness and inability to translate abstractions (like the definition of a sacrament as *an outward and visible sign of an inward and spiritual grace*), but I long to sense the spiritual grace of God's presence on the cellular level. Never mind the definitions. I want to see, touch, hear, feel it in the natural elements of creation.

Of course, God is more than those natural, tangible, visible, earthly elements, but there is a thread running through all of them that speaks of his creative presence. In the fragrance of late summer roses and the sound of water cascading into a pond . . . in a child's hand opened like a starfish . . . waiting for a gift . . . and the texture of chalk green lichen on a dying tree. You can't separate those elements from the "spiritual grace," can you? Matter matters.

Yet in the water of baptism there's something deeper . . . something even closer than the *creative presence* of God. I don't want to fall into the trap of the dark ages when the power of the sacraments bordered on idolatry. But the baptismal water is really an invitation to come . . . be *part of who I am*. St. Paul said, "It is no longer I who live but Christ who lives in me."[1] And when that happens . . . or as country singers say, "when I have Jesus in my bones" . . . it seems like we can feel *salvation* on the cellular level. Not just *God's presence* in the beauty of creation but *salvation* . . . something amazingly transformative. As in birthing, bathing, quenching, drowning, and breathlessly emerging from the deep. I guess that's why Delmar emerged from the river with a triumphant cry. And maybe why my grandson smiled.

And I guess that's why a few weeks ago on the first Sunday in Epiphany . . . I felt the lightest touch of the same sensibility. A couple in our congregation presented their child for baptism. Much to the obvious concern of the Altar Guild, the young minister poured a cascade of water into the font . . . letting it splash all over the floor. Then he took the child into his arms and poured the water over her head. In the name of the Father, the Son, and the Holy Spirit. And contrary to the practice of most ministers, he wasn't all that quick to dry her off.

But what was most surprising was that . . . after he presented the child to the congregation, he walked down the aisle and, taking a sprig of rosemary, he sprinkled us with the same water. Old men frowned and young women covered their eyes. But not me! I turned toward the aisle and waited my turn. "Let the water roll down my face. Let it wash all over me."

My enthusiasm was a bit surprising. But the older I get, the deeper my longing for the sacramental life. The more profound my desire to answer the invitation to be part of "who I am." I suppose it's the same for many who are in the second half of life. All too often our reservoir of gladness has been drained to almost empty. The one we loved is gone. A child is lost. A companion is reeling in the poison of his life. And we want something more than just seeing, touching, feeling the *creative presence* of God. We want to be *absorbed* in the creative presence of God's risen Christ.

And so we are.

It was a wonderful first Sunday in Epiphany. We heard the story of Jesus being baptized in the Jordan River. We witnessed the baptism of a little girl. And having experienced a mere sprinkling from a sprig of rosemary, I felt something new in the gladness of the afternoon. It would be a good day to walk down by the river.

Chapter 7

Expected Surprise

It was a beautiful evening . . . clear skies and the sweet smell of winter in the trees. The church was crowded. Mothers and fathers with restless children who stepped over each other so they could see. Solemn teenagers who promised not to text during the sermon. Grown children home for the holidays. Some were eager to see the place where they first heard the story of a babe lying in a manger. "Let's go to Bethlehem and see that which the Lord has made known to us."[1] Others were here just to please their parents (and their parents *were* pleased). Then, of course, there were the old folks who knew the traditions of the church and were holding on to them with white-knuckled tenacity.

We sang all the favorite hymns . . . about Mary, the mother of God, and Joseph, dearest Joseph. About the little Lord Jesus asleep on the hay and peace on earth, goodwill to everyone. I preached the miracle of the incarnation and people seemed satisfied. They said goodnight . . . gave me gifts . . . jars of homemade jam and pumpkin bread. Merry Christmas . . . merry Christmas.

I snuffed the candles and collected bulletins off the floor. Then I sat down in one of the front pews and listened to the echoes. We'd been preparing for this night a long time. With announcements from John the Baptist . . . prepare ye the way of the Lord.

And the archangel telling Mary that her child . . . the One she would bear . . . was the Son of God.

We sang "O Come, O Come Emmanuel" . . . and every week we sang another verse. Last Sunday the teachers presented a pageant. With lambs toddling down the aisle and wise men in bathrobes carrying gifts for the Christ child.

Then finally it was here. Christmas Eve.

But sitting there in the darkness, I thought . . . something was missing. For all the work, all the study, all the liturgy that had formed us in deep dispositions, something was missing. We'd been told that God would descend *unexpectedly* like "a thief in the night." But that's not really the way it was. We *knew* he was coming. It was on the calendar. December 25th. There was no surprise. No amazement.

And Christmas isn't some ordinary event. It's a towering miracle! The glorious Godhead of time and space leaves the realm of heaven and takes on human flesh. Not the flesh of a king or a prince but the flesh of a child born to young Jewish peasants. A throne for a stable? Power for weakness? As Gerard Manley Hopkins said, it was a "heaven-flung, heart-fleshed, maiden-furled, Miracle-in-Mary-of-flame."[2]

And yet it was also a solemn fact. A myth that happened. So where were the shepherds quaking at the sight?

I guess we knew too much. And I think as we've become so familiar with Christmas traditions that we've suffered what's called overfamiliarity, which can breed complacency. All the surprise is smothered out of existence. Is that possible?

I kept reflecting on what was missing, and in the solitude of the sanctuary I let my imagination roam . . . far out from our carefully designed pattern of worship. Why don't we celebrate Christmas again? Right now! Bring everyone back to church. "Let's go to Bethlehem and see that which the Lord has made known to us." We could ring huge peals of welcome in the tower bells (a carillon maybe). The organist could play another prelude

. . . this time with steel drums and wild percussions. And I wouldn't preach a sermon that merely *satisfied*. I'd lean out over the pulpit and tell everyone to "Wake up! Wake up! You've been asleep for two thousand years! And on this very night the Lord our God has come down from heaven to be with us . . . as a *real human being!*" That's all I would say . . . just "wake up!" What fun it would be . . . we could even have fireworks in the courtyard. (The worship committee would be horrified but I could depend on the children. Children love surprises.) It would be an evening full of excitement and joy. Of course, it wouldn't be one of unmitigated joy. There'd be counter testimonies hovering beneath the good news . . . things that we can't forget even for an hour. Our world, like that of Herod's, is flooded with violence. Refugees are streaming across the sands and even the joyful at home are stooped with sorrow. So maybe in this *cool, far-out* service we'd repeat some Advent prayers? Sing "O Come, O Come Emmanuel" one more time. That would be a *real* surprise. But we need for Christ to come again . . . we really do . . . like a thief in the night.

I left church after the clock had turned to another hour. There would be no fireworks, no bells pealing out a welcome, no Advent hymns. But there would be hope . . . always hope . . . that we would see the goodness of the Lord in the land of the living . . . again . . . and again. And I knew that in the deep darkness of the night I would wait with thousands of others for a towering miracle.

It would be a gracious surprise.

CHAPTER 8

What's in a Name?

A FEW DAYS AFTER OUR SECOND SON WAS BORN, A NURSE TOLD us that we had to give him a name. "Or we're going to register him in the courthouse records as 'No Name Engleby.'" We really didn't want our child to be called "No Name." Think of the taunts on the playground. But we also didn't want to call him by his father's, his grandfather's, and his great-grandfather's name. It would have been Joseph Thomas Engleby IV and that seemed like such a heavy burden for a seven pound baby boy. We named him Matthew Engleby instead.

Matt grew up with a heart full of both tenderness and mischief. He's now in Honduras where he works with a mission called El Hogar that rescues destitute children from the streets of Tegucigalpa. And I keep wondering if he would have missed that juncture in the road if he'd been named Joseph Thomas Engleby IV. Would he have felt obligated to follow the path of his lawyer father, grandfather, and great-grandfather? Names have a way of projecting expectations on a person.

I read a story about a young boy in the barrios of Los Angeles who wanted a name that would project the expectation of a tough guy in the street gangs. So he changed his name from Napoleon to Sniper. Father Gregory Boyle, Jesuit priest and author of *Tattoos on The Heart*, knew that Sniper wasn't his real name. "What's your

mom call you?" Napoleon hesitated. "Sometimes . . . sometimes
. . . when my mom's not mad at me . . . she calls me Napito."[1]

Names matter. They matter to moms, dads, grandfathers, and
great-grandfathers. They matter to nurses and children on the
playground.

Apparently they matter to God as well.

When Moses entered a pillar of cloud to complain about the
stiff-necked people, God said, "I will do the very thing that you
have asked; for you have found favor in my sight and I know you
by name."[2]

Really?

That idea seemed dubious to a young girl I met in New
Haven, Connecticut. Her father was very proud of her and one
day he told her to pray. "Go ahead, Emily. Show Jane how you
can pray like a big girl." And so she did. With a bell clear voice
for all the world to hear, she prayed. "Our Father, who art in New
Haven, how do you know my name?"

As always, I know that the "how" questions can never be
answered. But as St. Luke said, "Rejoice for your names are written in heaven."[3] Matthew. Matt. Napoleon. Napito. Emily. The
particularity of those names matters.

And the particularity of Jesus's name matters. Not "Jesus of
Nazareth" but the name that identified him on the day he was
baptized. Remember? When he emerged from the waters of
the Jordan River, a voice from heaven proclaimed, "You are my
Beloved. In you I am well pleased."[4]

"Beloved."

And since we have been made one with him in our own baptism, isn't Beloved *our* name as well? The first and deepest one we
have? Beloved Matthew, Beloved Matt, Beloved Napoleon, Beloved
Napito, Beloved Emily. It's a name that identifies us not only as
citizens born in a specific court district but as children of God.

And, of course, it follows that we would like to identify God
by name as well . . . in the manner of polite discourse. But on that

fateful day when God tells Moses to lead the people out of Egypt, Moses says, "If I go to the Israelites and tell them that the God of my ancestors has sent me and they ask, 'What's his name?' How shall I answer them?"

God tells Moses to say his name is "I AM WHO I AM."[5] Which isn't a name at all. It's the Great Divine Evasion. And I've always believed it was meant to stop us at the gate of know-ability and define-ability and control-ability. God is who God is so back off.

But maybe that's not what it's about. Maybe God meant for his name to have an alternate translation . . . one that doesn't say back off but says I WILL BE WHO I WILL BE as in a *promise*. A promise that one day . . . in the great by-and-by . . . we will know him fully. Our eyes will behold him and not as a stranger. And his name will be as real as our own.

That's a good promise.

But until that day, I'm going to keep on using the name that Jesus used when he spoke to God: Abba.

I'm sorry, Abba.

Abba, help me to live with gratitude . . . for everyone
Especially you.
Abba, please . . .
let my life bring forth life.
Even now.

It's Abba who hears my prayers. Hears mine and others. It's Abba who listens for the voice of children crying on the streets of Tegucigalpa. It's Abba who responds in a voice that Sniper remembers from his childhood.

"Hush . . . hush, Napito.
You are my Beloved."

CHAPTER 9

A Fence in the Rain

Why do I clip so many news articles? They just get stuffed away in a bottom drawer. It's a waste of time and space. So in my newly launched campaign to declutter, I decided to toss the whole drawer. Of course, I had to look through it first to make sure I wasn't tossing something important.

That was a tactical error. There were some very interesting articles in the drawer. One was about the seven year cycle of the gypsy moth. Another described Steven Spielberg's *Jurassic Park*. And another predicted that we would have computers the size of a watch within the decade. Really?

But there was one article that prompted me to read it again and think about it all afternoon. Suzanne Guthrie tells the story of a church meeting where all the excitement of the night was outside. A rainstorm was battering the roof and running down the gutters. Hundreds of scattered lights from the street lamp were reflected in parking lot puddles.

When the meeting ended, the adults lingered around the coffeepot to talk. But two teenagers slipped outside to wait for their rides. Everyone noticed. A loud crack against the roof announced another downpour, but the boy and girl . . . torn between a sensible retreat to shelter and the intrigue of the moment . . . decided to sit on a fence in the rain.[1]

The story reminded me of the time when my girlfriends and I were just as foolish. Sitting on a fence in the rain would have been an unexpected pleasure if it meant we could hold hands with our boyfriends. (Our parents couldn't possibly understand that the heavens had opened for us alone.)

Even as teenagers we knew what it was like to feel a longing in the soul to be understood and accepted. To share food and thoughts and words with someone who *liked* you. And, of course, to sense a somewhat fearful longing to be *known* in the biblical sense. Like Rodin's sculpture *The Kiss*, in which two lovers strain to embrace each other. The obvious longing to be *known* belies the cool metal of the medium.

And like the obvious longing expressed in the Song of Solomon, that naughty little book slipped into the canon between Ecclesiastes and Isaiah. The Songs breathe a delicious sensuality. "How much better is your love than wine; your lips distill nectar, my bride; . . . the scent of your garments is like the scent of Lebanon."[2]

Young love . . . it's so tender and hesitant. Like a fern unfurling in early spring.

But what young lovers will never believe is that when you're old and gray there's still a longing in the soul. Its urgency begins to mellow, of course. Instead of "sighing like a furnace" in the manner of Shakespeare's lover; instead of engaging in the pleasures of a scented darkness, old lovers take comfort in curling their tired limbs around each other. They sleep with a prayer for the other on their lips. And a murmured intention to engage again . . . perhaps in the morning.

It's all so beautiful.

But in a way I think old love has something that's better than young love. The longing has lasted long after the day we made a promise to love each other *forever*. And we have so many memories in our pocket . . . of rain falling on parking lot puddles, a sculpture that's warmer than its medium, the scent of pine on his wool jacket. There's something eternal about them. As William Butler Yeats once said:

> When you are old and grey and full of sleep,
> And nodding by the fire, take down this book,
> And slowly read, and dream of the soft look
> Your eyes had once, and of their shadows deep;
>
> How many loved your moments of glad grace,
> And loved your beauty with love false or true,
> But one man loved the pilgrim soul in you,
> And loved the sorrows of your changing face;
>
> And bending down beside the glowing bars,
> Murmur, a little sadly, how Love fled
> And paced upon the mountains overhead
> And hid his face amid a crowd of stars.[3]

Memories are no substitute for a kiss on the lips. But if my Love fled, maybe the memories would sustain me until the day I too paced upon the mountains overhead . . . and held in my arms the one I'll love forever.

The file drawer is still full of clippings. I threw out the articles about the gypsy moth and Steven Spielberg's *Jurassic Park*. But I put Guthrie's article back in the drawer. I'll probably never read it again but I know it's there to remind me of what it means to feel my soul awash with love. And, praise the Lord, I don't have to sit on a fence in the rain to enjoy it. The two of us can sit on the porch, watch it fall through the slender trees,

And pretend that the heavens have opened for us alone.

CHAPTER 10

The Wisdom of Clay

It was a hundred degrees in Baytown, Texas, that Sunday. The air was like a curtain blocking whatever breeze managed to slip through the windows at Trinity Episcopal Church. The ushers provided cardboard fans with a picture of the Last Supper on the back, but even with an image of Jesus the fans could barely move the air.

I was six years old . . . maybe seven . . . I can't remember. But my feet still didn't reach the floor so I kept swinging them beneath the pew. Back and forth. Back and forth. Until my grandmother reached over and put her hand on my knee. "Be still."

She wore white gloves every Sunday and carried a lace handkerchief to dab the perspiration from her face and neck. I tried to do the same thing with the hem of my dress but her hand came down again . . . swift and hard.

Then Mr. Hinkle began to preach. About John the Baptist. "I baptize you with water unto repentance: but he that cometh after me is mightier than I, whose shoes I am not worthy to carry: he shall baptize you with the Holy Ghost, and with *fire*."[1]

I had no idea what Mr. Hinkle was talking about but he talked a long time. Mopped his face and kept on preaching until finally it was over. We sang "Onward, Christian Soldiers" and said good-bye. Mr. Hinkle gave me a nice-girl pat on the head and we started home.

I asked a lot of questions on the way. "Is Jesus really going to baptize people with fire?" Won't it hurt? "Why wouldn't Mr. Hinkle carry Jesus's shoes?" My grandmother gave me less than satisfactory answers.

But yesterday I remembered that day in Baytown, Texas. The gospel for the day was the story of the Syrophoenician woman. She approaches Jesus as an unworthy stranger. Kneeling at his feet she begs him to heal her daughter. We expect Jesus to respond the way he usually does . . . with tender compassion. But he doesn't do that. He rebukes the woman. "It isn't fair to take the children's food and throw it to the dogs." The woman responds with the anguished challenge of a mother. "Even dogs under the table eat the children's crumbs."[2] Zing. Right to the sacred heart of Jesus.

He heals the child instantly, of course. And I have a vision of him lifting the woman to her feet in spite of the cultural impropriety of the gesture . . . thereby making her worthy to stand before him.

But having pondered the meaning of the gospel, having said the confession and celebrated the Eucharist with all its promise and gratitude, the congregation knelt down and recited one of its old traditional prayers: "We are not worthy so much as to gather up the crumbs under thy table." I wanted to stand up and say, "Wait a minute . . . didn't Jesus just *make* us worthy?" Isn't that the whole point of the story? He lifted the woman from a place where she was groveling in the dirt . . . to a place where she was worthy to stand before him. Isn't he doing the same for us? Lifting us to a place where we can feast with joy at the table with him?

I *wanted* to say all that, but remembering how my grandmother reached over to put her hand on my knee, I stayed still . . . kept my mouth shut. But what about our personhood? Are we or are we not worthy? And what about pride?

My answers have evolved again and again over time . . . ever since Mr. Hinkle gave me the impression, seeded by John the Baptist, that I wasn't worthy enough to carry Jesus's shoes . . . to yesterday when I felt a protest rising from my heart . . . about to break from my lips.

Rob Bell says the truth "is like a pool you dive into, and you start swimming toward the bottom, and soon you discover that no matter how hard and fast you swim downward, the pool keeps getting . . . deeper. The bottom will always be out of reach."[3]

But no matter . . . I keep swimming . . . swimming toward the bottom . . . trying to understand who and what we are as human beings in relationship to God. Especially when it comes to women who've been humiliated as strangers from other cultures.

If in the beginning God said, "Let us make humankind in our image, according to our likeness." And having said that, God picked up the dust of the ground and molded us into little clay models of himself, then we must be worth *something*. The divine image has been scarred and blemished through years of faithless living, but surely it's not obliterated.

And again, in the deep compassion of God in Christ we have been raised, lifted up and given a place at the table. Not that we should brag about it! We didn't find a place at the table because we were self-made worthies . . . barging in like uninvited guests. We found a place at the table because we were *made* worthy! We were *invited* to the table. And we approach it with humility . . . hat in hand.

So I guess I'll keep on struggling with the issue. I'm thinking, however, that when I reach the end of *my* journey I'll see Jesus strolling along the beach at Emmaus. I'll catch up with him . . . walk side by side in the rippled sand and look for shells buried in the tides. And maybe I'll be bold enough to say, "Can I carry your shoes?" My guess is that Jesus will turn to me and say, "Why, yes, indeed. And thank you very much."

CHAPTER 11

Semantic Slippage

CONFIRMATION CLASSES WERE SO BORING. ESPECIALLY ON SUNday afternoon when I wanted to be outside with my friends . . . playing Kick the Can. I had to learn the Ten Commandments, the Summary of the Law, the Lord's Prayer, and the definition of grace, covenant, sacrament, and the impossible Trinity. Then I had to explain why we were an *apostolic church*. But the hardest lesson of all was memorizing the Nicene creed . . . every line. I believe that . . . I believe that . . . I believe that . . . and so on.

But eventually I could give the correct answers (except for the impossible Trinity). And I could even recite the Nicene creed. So the good bishop laid his heavy hands on my head. "Defend, O Lord, this your child with thy heavenly grace that she may continue thine forever." I had arrived. No more classes. Maybe no more church?

I can still remember the night of my confirmation . . . when the games and baths were done. I was lying in my bed by the window and something bothered me . . . like a mosquito whining around my ear. Did God really care if I knew all that stuff?

My adolescent angst was probably due to the word itself . . . *belief.* Over the years it suffered serious semantic slippage. Originally it meant the same thing as a vow, a promise, a commitment. I give my heart, my loyalty, my devotion to the One who died, was buried, and was raised from the dead. You believed *in* instead of believing *that* . . . as in church doctrines. Not that doctrines weren't important. They were very important . . . especially as deterrents to curly headed heresies.

But at the core of it all *belief* wasn't about intellectual assent. It was about a Person. As Marcus Borg said in *Speaking Christian*, "To believe meant not only confidence and trust in a person . . . it also meant to hold that person dear . . . to *belove* that person."[1] Of course, in the intellectual atmosphere of seminary we spoke of God as the "ground of being" or the "transcendent absolute." And it's a bit hard to *belove* a "ground of being" or a "transcendent absolute."

But long after my seminary days I heard a story about St. John of the Cross. He often stayed at a convent over Christmas. And one time . . . late at night . . . a sister observed him doing something very strange. He went to the chapel and leaned over the cradle where the figure of the Christ child lay. When he thought no one was looking, he picked up the figure and hugged it close to his heart. Then, with his eyes closed, he danced around the crib.

St. John *beloved* the Christ child.

Unfortunately, we live in a culture that thinks the image of a monk dancing around a crib is silly . . . he's a little dotty. But isn't that what it's all about? Being dotty? Especially in our later years when we can't explain the doctrines? Does God really care if I don't understand the impossible Trinity?

I think I *want* to be a little dotty. I want to dance around the crib. I want to be smitten, God-enthralled.

And if I'm not? If I'm lapsing into negligence, forgetting my prayers, failing in my ministries? Will I no longer continue "thine forever"? No more "heavenly grace"? That's what I was asking myself when, quite unannounced, the ghost of a good bishop slipped into the room.

It was as if he were trying to tell me the same thing he told me when I was thirteen years old. "Of course, God will continue to defend you with his heavenly grace. *Beloving* isn't some *quid pro quo* deal. You can never match God's side of the equation. His love is a 'sign of the covenant' deal. It's a 'you're marked as Christ's own forever' deal. It's an embrace. So go back to your books and study the doctrines you had to memorize years ago. Write their meanings in your *heart*."

And so I began to believe *that*. Not altogether, but bit by bit I began to believe *that* my trespasses would be forgiven; *that* God's covenant would never be broken; *that* in spite of my woeful human apathy, I would "continue thine forever." Strangely enough . . . believing *in* and believing *that* were somehow reconciled.

Only a few days later I heard the sound of wind tossing the branches of our big oak tree . . . it was a deep hum like that of a cello's strings . . . and it seemed to invite my feet to move. Back and forth. Side to side. In a soft shoe dance . . . letting my skirt follow in rhythmic waves of joy.

If anyone had seen me they would have said I was silly. That "dotty old woman." And without missing a beat, I would have acknowledged the compliment.

And kept on dancing
until the music was over.

CHAPTER 12

To Clap or Not to Clap?

ONE SATURDAY YEARS AGO I TOOK KATE AND SALLY, OUR TWO young daughters, to New York to see *Peter Pan*. This was before the era of bold theatrical tricks, so we were quite surprised when Peter Pan flew across the stage and out over the audience. He was right above our heads! (Of course, he was suspended from an invisible wire, but still, as far as we were concerned, Peter Pan was flying.)

But the best part of the play was after Tinker Bell almost died. And Peter Pan ran to the edge of the stage and begged the audience, "Please, clap for her! Clap real hard and she'll know you want her to live." So, of course, we clapped and clapped. I looked over at Kate and Sally and they were not only clapping, they were crying. So I cried. And there we were, wishing Tinker Bell back to life with our hands and our tears.

And it worked! Slowly her wings began to flutter . . . struggling with a glow that seemed to come from within and without. Then she rose up out of the darkness and began flying right next to Peter Pan. She was alive! It was a wonderfully sentimental miracle.

But I've prayed for the same miracle time and time again. Hoping that a friend who was fading from life would live. It worked sometimes. Just the way it worked for Tinker Bell. But on other occasions it didn't. So why pray? What difference does it make if I clap or don't clap?

I guess I've always thought of prayer as a conversation that would produce *results*. If I prayed hard enough, the door would open and all the resources of God's grace would pour forth for my benefit.

But that's not always true.

There's a rather irreverent passage about that question in *Huckleberry Finn*. It goes something like this:

Miss Watson, she told me to pray every day and whatever I asked for I would get. But it warn't so. I tried it. Once I got a fish line but no hooks. It warn't any good without the hooks. I tried for the hooks three or four times but somehow I couldn't make it work.

By and by one day I asked Miss Watson to try for me but she said I was a fool. She never told me why. I says to myself, if a body can get anything they pray for, why don't Deacon Winn get back the money he lost in pork. Why can't the widow get back the silver snuff box that was stole. Why can't Miss Watson fatten up. No, I says to myself, there ain't nothing in it.[1]

Huck was on to something. No matter how hard we pray . . . no matter how long we kneel on the hardwood floor or beat our fists against the wall, some prayers don't produce *results*. At least not the results we were hoping for. Paul prayed that the thorn would be removed from his side but it wasn't. Jesus prayed that the cup would pass from his lips and it didn't.

So again . . . why pray?

Someone asked C. S. Lewis the same question shortly after he had prayed for his wife to live and she hadn't lived. His answer? "I can't *not* pray." Apparently, having practiced prayer over a lifetime, the discipline was grafted in his bones. And he couldn't live without it. Even in the darkest hour the struggle to find meaning continued.

The same was true of Elie Wiesel. He tells the story of how he and his fellow prisoners at Auschwitz cried out against the Eternal Lord of the Universe. "One day they decided to put him on trial . . . if God was omnipotent, he could have prevented the Shoah; if he could not stop it, he was impotent; and if he could have stopped it but chose not to, he was a monster. They condemned God to death. The All Powerful and Terrible One is *dead*. The presiding rabbi pronounced the verdict then went on calmly to announce that it was time for evening prayer."[2]

The discipline of prayer was grafted in their bones.

But I wonder if maybe there was something more than discipline pulling them to their knees. I wonder if maybe there's a universal instinct within each of us. One that we can't suppress? ("I can't not pray.") A longing to be in touch with the transcendent? Not as a means to an end, but simply to be in touch with.

One night recently I stayed a long time in the memory place thinking about that day in New York. I could enter Peter Pan's hopeful imagination as if it were today instead of years ago. I could see the girls . . . now grown and with children of their own. I could even see their dresses and the stage and the whole audience clapping. And not only that . . . I could see people standing outside on Broadway clapping! And even beyond them there was clapping. It was like a fire that picks up with the wind. Even the saints were gathered in its sweep. Saint Andrew and Saint Luke started clapping. And Saint Sebastian . . . with all the arrows in his sides . . . began to clap. So did Thomas Aquinas.

It was a huge circle that expanded all the way back to the hands that had been nailed to the cross. I wanted to be in touch with them . . . put my palms between those palms. And in that momentary vision that comes just before you fall asleep, I could see a pair of wings struggling with a glow that seemed to come from within and without. Then they broke free . . .

and rose up out of the darkness.
As if beyond the trappings of time
there was an eternity.

CHAPTER 13

Ringing Them Home

THERE WAS AN OLD STEEPLE BELL IN MY HOME CHURCH. IT WAS way up in the tower and as a child I was quite curious about it. The sound had such power, such resonance. I could feel it in my belly. One Sunday the minister said I could go up with Warden Jones and ring the bell. Me? Ring the bell? "Yes," he said. "Go on now. It's time." So Warden Jones and I climbed the wooden steps . . . round and round and round . . . until we reached the top of the tower.

And there it was . . . a huge bell aged with patina. Mr. Jones handed me the rope and said I should ring it. I tried . . . tugged as hard as I could. It wouldn't move. But finally . . . with a little help from Mr. Jones . . . it began to swing. Out and back, out and back. And then . . . much to my delight . . . I was lifted up off my feet . . . ringing and swinging in the early morning sun.

I could see people down below. They were unloading children from the car, helping grandfathers cross the street, and chatting with friends. But as the sound of the bell grew louder, they began to hurry. A lady lost her hat. She had to pick it up off the street and run to catch up.

I would have kept on ringing and swinging all day, but Mr. Jones said, "That's enough. They're gathered now." And when I went back down the wooden steps, I saw that, sure enough, the church was full. Everyone was in place waiting to sing the opening hymn.

Looking back on that Sunday morning, I realize that ringing the bell was my first effort at evangelism. I was summoning people to church. "Hurry! This is where you'll hear good news."

I had responded to the same summons for most of my life . . . primarily out of habit. We went to church on Sundays . . . we just did. The habit began to wear thin in my adulthood. Often the liturgy seemed dry and disembodied. Sermons didn't offer much in the way of spiritual protein. And the announcements were endless. So instead of confessing on bended knee and praising God with all my heart and soul and mind and strength, I'd drift away . . . think about the grocery list. (Don't forget to buy more laundry soap.)

And there were times when I drifted away altogether. It was sort of nice. I could stay home on Sundays, sleep late, and maybe have a big breakfast of scrambled eggs and biscuits.

But it's curious . . . because even as I drifted, I felt as if I were on a tether. Like an astronaut floating above the surface of the earth. And eventually I'd feel a tug at my soul. "Jane, you've gone far enough. It's time to come home." And I'd return . . . landing feet first on familiar ground.

I don't drift that much anymore. It's probably due to wobbly knees and senile vertigo. But for whatever reason, wandering makes me nervous. I usually stick close to home. The choir is slightly less than perfect. The speaker system is weak so I may or may not hear the sermon . . . which may or may not be a good thing. And the announcements are still endless. But it's where I belong. And it seems foolish to expect the church to fit my expectations perfectly. So when I hear the bell, I hurry home.

There are a lot of drifters who *never* hurry home. Some are angry because God's face seems set against them. Some are cynical. "You churchy people are just interested in rules and creeds. All that institutional stuff!" And some totally misunderstand what the church is all about. They hear the raging claims of soul snatching

Christians. "If you don't come back to church . . . when the Lord gathers up the souls of the faithful, you won't be with them." No wonder they stay away.

For the longest time I didn't worry about those people. It's *their* loss. "You can keep on floating if that's what you like!" But now that I worship in a half-empty church where prayers echo off the walls, I realize that it's *our* loss as well. Without them the community isn't complete. It's like a jigsaw puzzle with a missing piece of the pale blue sky. And seeing the emptiness makes me want to climb up wooden steps and ring a steeple bell again. "Come home! We need you! We need your energy, your voice. We need your crazy new ideas."

I'll tell them how nice it is to have the fellowship of coffee hours and potluck suppers. To have friends who share the happy times. And how comforting it is to have them in times of crisis when your knees buckle under the weight of grief.

But I'll also tell them that there's something much more compelling about church. Much more meaningful than coffee hour and potluck fellowship. I'll tell them that when we respond to the bell, we're doing it because our deep desire to be in personal communion with God is completed in our communion with one another. Jesus taught his disciples to pray *Our* Father, not *My* Father. I'll remind them of that.

And even though they may often feel a deep longing for physical solitude . . . a wilderness of the Spirit . . . away from the chatter of voices, they need to come back home and celebrate . . . with a party. Sharing a banquet where thousands of grains of wheat are gathered to form one loaf of bread.

That's what I need to tell the drifters.

And maybe I'll even climb up those old wooden steps . . . round and round and round . . . until I reach the top of the tower. Then I could ring the bell . . . call out to people below, "Hurry! It's time to come home. We're having a party."

I hope there'll be a Mr. Jones to help me.

CHAPTER 14

Lettuce in the Lap

THE SNOW HAD BEEN FALLING FOR DAYS. IT WOULD THAW IN THE noonday sun leaving an icy crust. Aunt Mimi had flown east that week to see Tommy, my young husband who was dying of cancer. When she stepped out of the car, she slipped and her ankle snapped. Broken on a crust of ice. I took her to the hospital where they wrapped her foot in a plaster cast. Then we went home where she shared a room upstairs with our girls.

But I was young then. I could take care of the sick as well as the injured. No problem. And I could take care of our four children who were, like me, hanging on a filament of hope.

Then one night I fixed a salad for the invalids. A beautiful salad with French dressing and a garnish of Gorgonzola cheese. But just as I started up the stairs, I tripped. Avocados and grapefruit were scattered across the wool carpet, mixed together with dirt and dog hair.

And what did I do? Clean it up? Start over? No. I sat there with lettuce in my lap and yelled at the ceiling. "I can't do it anymore!! Do you hear? I can't do it anymore."

Now, I had been raised a good Episcopalian and you definitely didn't speak to God that way. When you spoke to God, you said things like "we beseech thee" and "thou who didst give thine only-begotten son." You were supposed to be *nice* when you spoke to God.

But I wasn't feeling *nice* that snowy evening. I was feeling abandoned. Jesus said, "Come to me, all you who are weary and burdened, and I will give you rest."[1] So where the heck was he?

I still look back on that evening and wonder how/why things happened the way they did. Was there a connection between Mimi's broken ankle and my broken spirit? Spiritual advisors urge surrender as the way of the pilgrim soul. "One must relinquish a totally unreliable faith in the self for a totally reliable faith in God." Good advice, but my surrender had nothing to do with a moral decision or pious abdication. I just couldn't do it anymore.

Neither could my young husband. He died a few weeks later. We commended him to Almighty God . . . earth to earth, ashes to ashes, dust to dust. We planted some jonquils at the head of his grave and tried to move on. I wrote letters. Paid the bills. Fed the children. Aunt Mimi called often to see how we were doing. I managed life as best I could.

But often the weeks that followed once more took the shape of anger and frustration. I wanted to pound my fists against heaven's gate. Yell at the ceiling again. If I'd been able to summon the courage, I might have voiced my complaints more forcefully. The way the psalmists did.

God, you're my last chance of the day . . .
I'm camped on the edge of hell.
You've dropped me into the bottomless pit
Sunk me in a pitch black abyss . . .
For as long as I remember I've been hurting;
I've taken the worst you can hand out, and I've had it.
You made lover and neighbor alike dump me.

The only friend I have left is darkness.[2]

I would never have the courage to speak *that* forcefully. But I have to admit . . . the psalmists didn't suffer in silence. They voiced their complaints with as much candor as they voiced their praise . . . insisting in a way that sharing everything with God was an act of faith.

Besides . . . that day I sat with lettuce in my lap . . . I felt a strange sense of relief. As if God were *embracing* my anger. Not *rejecting* it but *embracing* it. And in the unspoken space beyond the words, something changed. I don't know what it was. My attention? God's attention? A combination? It's strange but . . . as with the psalms . . . the very fact of depositing anguish and anger at the feet of God, prompted a movement . . . a click of the compass from feeling abandoned to feeling compassion.

Not that it reversed the course of life and death. It didn't. But at least my voice hadn't vaporized. It hadn't been recorded on an answering machine. Or merged into nothingness. And . . . it was amazing . . . I could feel a brooding presence hovering over the stairs.

It was weeks later . . . a morning in early spring . . . when I looked out the window and I could see the wind lift the snow off the sycamore tree. The mountain beyond was still pale in the early dawn. But it was enough for me to whisper what broken spirits often whisper . . . "Alleluia anyway."

CHAPTER 15

Too Deep for Words

I'VE ALWAYS THOUGHT PRAYERS WOULD BECOME MORE MEAN-
ingful as I got older. I'd pour out my heart with pleadings and
praise until the very words caught fire. "O Lord, how excellent
are thy ways." But somehow that's not what's happened. More
often than not, these days my prayers are just a mumble of rote
memory. Maybe it's because I'm travel weary ... such a long road
to this stage in life. Or maybe it's because I've entered what they
call a *dry season.*

I learned to pray when I was very young. Kneeling beside
my grandmother, I rolled the phrases off my lips. "We have left
undone those things which we *ought* to have *done,* and we have
done those things which we *ought* not to have *done!*" My grandmother said I should use the Book of Common Prayer. That's
where we could find the proper words to use when we spoke to
God. (Episcopalians are into propriety.)

I learned to love the language: "Christ our Passover is sacrificed
for us, therefore let us keep the feast; Not with the old leaven, but
with the unleavened bread of sincerity and truth." In the 1970s they
modernized the book, but the new one was still quite beautiful ...
the absence of *thous* and *whatsoevers* notwithstanding.

I even tried to translate some of the words for our deaf congregation, willing my hands to sign what sound conveyed to the

hearing. I did fine with "let us pray," and "thanks be to God." But one Sunday . . . feeling rather proud of my expanding vocabulary . . . I signed, "The peace of the Lord be with you." Only to discover later that what I had actually signed wasn't "the peace of the Lord be with you," but "the hamburger of the Lord be with you."

I wonder if God laughed.

And yet as time passed, even the new language began to sound routine, worn mute from overuse. I could still roll the words off my lips, but instead of rising like a song off the page, they fell like dried leaves in autumn. There was a disconnect . . . a sad sense of absence from the One on the other end of the line.

Other prayer books were available. New collections were published every month . . . offering candid expressions of gratitude, guilt, sorrow, and so forth. Some were elegantly dressed. Others were clothed in simplicity . . . like the one offered in Rumi's story "Moses and the Shepherd."

God, where are you? I want to help you, to fix your shoes and comb your hair, to wash your clothes and pick the lice off. I want to bring you milk and kiss your little hands and feet when it's time for you to go to bed. I want to sweep your room and keep it neat. God, my sheep and goats are yours. All I can say remembering you is aye and aaah.[1]

Such a tender expression of love . . . a feast with the unleavened bread of sincerity and truth. And the prayer was expectant . . . longing not just to rattle off the proper words but to receive a response in the conversation.

I decided to cobble together a few prayers in the same colloquial voice (without mention of lice). "Hello, God. I've really missed talking to you! Could you . . . like . . . come sit next to me. We could share a glass of iced tea and . . . are you there?"

For some reason my prayers weren't that effective. There was still a disconnect. Like the shepherd boy, I began to wonder, "God, where are you?"

Then late one August afternoon I was arranging wildflowers in a vase that belonged to my grandmother, and I remembered how sometimes she'd tell me to be quiet. "Shhhhh!" Could that be the problem? I'd learned how to talk to God . . . big time . . . but maybe I'd been talking too much. (It's a fatal habit of old age.) Maybe God was waiting for me to take a breath. He would never interrupt me . . . I know that. An interruption would take away the freedom he had given me.

But if I truly believed the words of the prayers that I had been saying all those years, then God was not absent. God was out there somewhere . . . hidden but not hiding. And he *wanted* to enter a conversation with me. Maybe more than I did. "Be still and know that I am your God."

I put down the wildflowers and looked out the window. Beyond the porch and the garden and the trees there was a meadow . . . open to the skies. It looked like a cloth spread out for weary travelers. A place to rest. So I left the house, walked up through the dry grasses and lay down.

It was so quiet. Even the katydids stopped hopping. I felt as if there was something more than the absence of sound in the meadow. I drifted off to sleep and woke up later when clouds were gathering over the mountains.

Maybe someday I'll learn that what they call a dry season isn't dry at all. It's part of the journey. And eventually . . . down the long road . . . the thirst for a deeper communion is so strong we can no longer roll the words off our lips. And God . . . having waited for a long time . . . moves into the stillness and showers us with a summer rain.

CHAPTER 16

Why the Cross?

WE SANG "ROCK OF AGES" IN CHURCH THIS MORNING. WE NEVER sing "Rock of Ages" so it was a pleasant surprise to let the words roll out of our tuneful hearts.

Rock of ages, cleft for me,
Let me hide myself in thee;
. . .
In my hand no price I bring,
simply to thy cross I cling.[1]

There's a big wooden cross outside my home church. I can still see it . . . rising up out of the garden . . . rough-hewn from old wooden beams. And I can still remember taking our grandchildren there for a wedding reception.

They behaved fairly well at first. The boys kept their shirts tucked in; the girls kept their sashes tied. But after a while they got restless and started chasing each other around the garden. Strange, incongruous words bounced off the walls. "You're it." "Gotcha." "Last tag." The game was in full swing when one of the girls ran across the garden and wrapped her arms around the big wooden cross. "You can't get me now," she cried. "I'm safe here."

And so she was. But beyond the game of tag the cross doesn't keep us safe, does it? There are too many "gotchas" in life. And whenever that not-so-safe feeling slips up on me, I can't help wondering *why the cross?*

Maybe God meant for Jesus to live a long and fruitful life . . . establish a few churches, go on mission trips, and so on. Then when he was full of years, ascend to heaven like Elijah in a chariot of fire. But that's not what the political and religious leaders had in mind. They said "Crucify him!" So they did. And for years the church tried to justify the scandal by saying it was meant for our redemption. "All glory be to thee our heavenly Father for thou didst give thine only Son Jesus Christ to suffer death upon the cross for our redemption, a full, perfect and sufficient sacrifice for the sins of the whole world."[2]

I've heard those words so often . . . every Sunday and then some . . . and I've always assumed that was the *why of the cross.* It was a sacrifice to God for our sins. But lately . . . in the afterthoughts of age . . . I'm haunted by the suggestion that the God I love and worship is an angry dictator . . . demanding some sort of payment to satisfy his idea of justice? And the payment is the innocent Jesus. "A full, perfect, and sufficient sacrifice for the sins of the whole world."

It doesn't make sense. Why couldn't intercessions on our behalf be effective without Jesus having to be tortured and killed? Imagine having to explain that *why* to children. There they are in the Sunday school room . . . sitting on little painted chairs. And as the teacher you say, "See, children, Jesus was the son of God and his father (God) loved the world so much that he sent Jesus to die on the cross for our sins because . . . well, it's like this . . . someone had to pay for all the bad things we had done and God decided . . ."

"Wait a minute," says the towheaded kid in the front row. "You mean God killed his son?! Why would he do that? My daddy wouldn't do that to me." The explanation would probably leave some damage in its wake. "Our Father who art in heaven, I wish you hadn't sent Jesus to be killed."

The whole sacrificial idea is troubling. Which is probably why singing "Rock of Ages" was so refreshing for me. "In my hand no price I bring, simply to thy cross I cling."

But still the question stands. If not a sacrifice, *why the cross?* Why is such a brutal event redemptive?

I remember thinking the same thing on a visit to England's Coventry Cathedral (destroyed in the firebomb blitz of 1940). I was walking through the empty shell when I saw a cross that had been recovered from the ashes. It wasn't made of burnished brass or polished silver. It was made of charred timbers.

I looked at it for the longest time and even though I was surrounded by ruins, I felt a sense of grace. "Surely the Lord is in this place." And if surely in a *place* of defeat, then surely in a *life* of defeat. Isn't that what he meant when he took on flesh and became one with us? And not just *us* as in a general proclamation . . . but *me* as in a personal proclamation. "Rock of ages, cleft for me, Let me hide myself in thee."

As Alister McGrath said, "the hands that flung the stars into the heavens were surrendered to the nails of the cross."[3] Blessed is the One who would do such a thing for the whole world . . . and for me.

I guess that explains the *why of the cross* . . . somewhat. When laughter ripples through the garden, God is there. But when life seems like an empty shell, God is also there. And maybe even closer to us . . . sensing that it's where we are most in need.

But that doesn't mean we no longer have to suffer. It's the other way around, isn't it? God identifies with us through the cross of Jesus Christ because we *do* have to suffer. It's part of the human condition.

I wish it were otherwise.

But suffering isn't the end of the story. Isn't the post-Easter insight a revelation of God leading us through the empty shell?

In the words of Isaiah, "I have taken you by the hand. When you pass through the ruins I will be with you."[4]

And so that day in Coventry, I reached out for a hand to lead me. Past the rubble of broken bricks and burnt timbers. Past the threshold of defeat. Until finally we reached the doors of a new cathedral. And there on a wall at the far end of the sanctuary was a tapestry of brilliant colors. Reds, yellows, blues, the greens of early spring. And in the middle of all that magnificence was an image of Christ in Glory . . . towering over the wrecks of time.

I'm still trying to understand *why the cross*. And I'm beginning to think it isn't something you can understand from the outside . . . from books, papers, lectures, the scribbling of an old woman. It's something you can only understand from the inside . . . by taking the hand that leads you to a new place. Sometimes it's an understanding

      that runs so deep,

          it makes you tremble, tremble, tremble.

CHAPTER 17

The Bible Tells Me So

THERE'S A PRAYER ABOUT HOW THE HOLY SCRIPTURES ARE written for our learning and how we should read, mark, learn, and inwardly digest them. I started doing all that when I was a child at my grandmother's house. She would read stories from her Bible, and I would ask questions. "How does God stay up there?" "Did Jonah see Pinocchio in the belly of the whale?"

Then at Sunday school we painted pictures of Noah's Ark and looked for the Holy Land on worn out wall maps. At Christmas the boys walked down the aisle carrying something the teacher said was frankincense. And the girls . . . in their angel wings . . . hovered over the manger. It was active learning. We didn't understand the Bible. We experienced it. As Paul said, "I fed you with milk, not solid food, for you were not ready for solid food."[1]

My first grown-up Bible class didn't provide much more in the way of solid food. It was sort of like a trampoline. The teacher would introduce a passage and then she'd ask how we felt that day. At which point we'd leap off the page into a discussion of our personal lives. All of which was quite therapeutic; it brought us together as a support group, but it didn't help us read, mark, learn, and inwardly digest Holy Scriptures.

A few ambitious friends decided the best way to do that was to read the Bible on their own, from cover to cover. But as Peter

Gomes said in his classic *The Good Book*, "those who get through usually feel as if they have run a marathon, where the object of the course is to finish and not necessarily to observe the landscape along the way. Those who do not cross the finish line often feel like moral failures who have broken their diet or fallen off the wagon and taken a forbidden drink."[2]

I never had the discipline to try a marathon, but when seminary professors introduced me to a critical study of the Bible, I began to observe the landscape along the way. Apparently the book had been generated through human beings with all their passions and idiosyncrasies. Some passages were more "reliable" than others. Some were more "original." Some more "accurate." And all of them were "culturally conditioned."

It made me a little nervous. But the professors said that the greatest thinkers of modern times had done the research, and if I ignored it, I would remain "landlocked in an uncritical naiveté." No one wants to be landlocked in uncritical naiveté. So I cruised through the open waters of history, liturgy, subtexts, and parallels.

It was a lot to inwardly digest. And sometimes . . . with so many verses scattered across the desk . . . I wanted to hit the reverse button . . . let them all go backward like dry leaves lifting off the ground and returning to the branches . . . all green again. As President Grover Cleveland once said, "The Bible is good enough for me, just the old book under which I was brought up. I do not want notes or criticisms or explanations about authorship or origins or even cross-references. I do not need them or understand them, and they confuse me."[3]

I could appreciate the president's feelings. When we speak of "the authority of scripture" do we mean it should stand on its own without "critics"? Is it a sacrilege to poke our noses into this complex combination of the divine and human? Or have we been given the capacity to interpret for some divine reason? It's a troubling conflict.

But no matter . . . I couldn't go back. I couldn't go back to a landlocked naiveté. It was too late. And the more I studied the original context of the words . . . with all their passions and idiosyncrasies . . . the more the Bible began to seem like a "living text." Not history or a remnant of the past that happened once but never again. The words are fixed on the page but *something* animated them and drew me into a deeper consideration of our relationship to God. As the writer of Hebrews said, "Indeed the word of God is living and active, sharper than any two edged sword, piercing until it divides soul from spirit, joints from marrow."[4] As far as I was concerned, the critical research *was* the two edged sword. It allowed the Spirit to take the original context and bring it forward to *my* context.

And *my* context has changed a lot over the years. I remember the first time I read Luke's story of the sinful woman bathing Jesus's feet with her tears. And I thought *wow* . . . what an extravagant gesture of love (and rather erotic). But according to the law of Leviticus, Jesus was allowing himself to be *defiled*. The Pharisee host condemned him for a failure of "righteousness." "Did he not know who and what kind of woman this is who is touching him?"[5]

Something pulled me into a deeper consideration of the story's meaning. What does righteousness mean? What does it mean to be a Pharisee? Who knows what else I'll discover in the living text? Maybe I'll learn over and over again the story of extravagant love.

In the meantime I'm going to put my grandmother's Bible near my bed.

The leather cover is cracked with age.
Names on the index thumbs
have disappeared as if no longer needed.
My grandmother knew
where Jeremiah was.

Between the pages there's a summer flower
pressed to remember
a transient season of delight.
The red lettered words of Jesus
have preserved a beauty in its leaving.

Then when I'm *really* old, I'll take it out, hold it in my hands, and let it tell me everything from the beginning, when the earth was without form and void, to the ending when all will be gathered into one. I'll let it tell me the story of people coming into the nearness of God and understanding how they were meant to live as human beings. I'll let it tell me how I can endure the shocks the flesh is heir to and cope with my mortality.

I may even press another summer flower between its pages—an evening primrose, perhaps. It will remind me of how Sarah was told she would bear new life in her old age. She laughed at the absurdity of God's grace but a season of delight began to bloom again.

CHAPTER 18

Wellspring of Gratitude

IT WAS MONEY SUNDAY ... A REGULAR FALL EVENT WHERE THE church presses members to make financial commitments to the treasury. The gospel was from Mark ... the one about rich people putting money in the treasury. Glancing this way and that to see if others were watching, they deposit a stack of gold coins on the table.

Jesus is sitting nearby and when a poor widow comes and puts two small copper pennies in the plate, he says, "Truly I tell you, this poor widow has put in more than all those who are contributing to the treasury. For they have contributed out of their abundance; but she out of her poverty has put in everything she had, all she had to live on."[1]

Over the years I've heard a lot of sermons about those hypocritical rich people. "They will receive the greater condemnation for their puffed up pride and vain hypocrisy." As a preacher lady, I've even made some of those suggestions myself.

But now that I'm older, I take a more practical approach. Instead of condemning them, I say, "Bring it on! Put that stack of gold coins on the table! Put hundred dollar bills in the collection plate! And don't worry about your righteousness. We'll work on that next week."

It would be a breach of church propriety to say that, of course. But when you're my age, breaching propriety is sort of a privilege.

And yet on this particular Money Sunday I was pulled into a deeper and disturbing question. How could that poor widow have put everything she had in the plate? How did she pay her bills? Repair the leak in her roof? How did she . . . like so many who live in abject poverty . . . find a scrap of food to feed her children?

Did she sit on the side of the road like the widow of Zarephath and beg? "As the Lord our God lives, I have only a handful of meal in a jar and a little oil in a jug."[2]

And you get the impression that the poor widow wasn't dropping copper pennies into the plate out of *obligation*. Like . . . "I have to support the operating budget." There was even something joyful in the way she gave everything away. How in the world did such generosity rise up out of such poverty?

There's a sense of unreality in the situation. And yet. I've seen it before.

We were in Honduras a few years ago . . . visiting a mission that shelters hundreds of desperate children in the capital of Tegucigalpa. They call it El Hogar, which means "the home." The children come from gang-infested streets and houses made out of cardboard and tin. Often their only meal is picked morsel by stale morsel from garbage cans. El Hogar's mission is to rescue them, feed them, heal them, teach them, and bring hope back into their lives.

As visitors that year, we went to Sunday mass with the children. A volunteer sitting next to one of them pulled a Hershey bar out of her bag and gave it to the child. A whole Hershey bar wrapped in glossy brown paper. The boy hardly knew what to do with it. He kept turning it over and over in his hands. Tracing the silver letters. Hershey. Chocolate.

You'd think that when mass was over he'd taste and see that it was good. But he didn't do that. Instead, he stepped into the center aisle where everyone was walking out of church. He peeled away the glossy brown paper and tin foil. Then he carefully broke off each chocolate square. And gave them . . . one by one . . . to children in the aisle.

The body of Christ.

In the dark recesses of poverty, both the boy and the widow seemed to have discovered an ultimate truth. The copper pennies and chocolate candy were gifts. Indeed, everything was a gift . . . clean clothes, water, toothbrushes, corn for supper, a little oil in a jug. Everything.

Imagine such an epiphany. And in its wake I don't think either the widow or the boy could *not* have given all they had. So powerful was the gratitude rushing from the wellspring of their hearts. You couldn't put a stopper on it. Especially if you worshiped the Giver of the gifts.

O, to be so grateful in my waning years . . . for fading roses and copper pennies. For the long green days that are left for us to live.

For a handful of meal in a jar.

And for a candy bar wrapped in glossy brown paper.

CHAPTER 19

Yes behind the No

HE WAS AN HONEST YOUNG PREACHER. HANDSOME, TOO. DARK hair falling across his forehead. Hands that trembled slightly when he turned the pages. And his sermon was good . . . delivered with scholarly references and a few homespun illustrations. But his text was the Binding of Isaac and whenever that text is part of the lectionary, I suffer an immediate aversion to God's word.

It's in Genesis 22. God says to Abraham, "Take your son, your only son, Isaac, whom you love, and go to the land of Moriah and offer him there as a burnt offering."

Not only does the demand violate a sacred bond between father and son, it violates God's own faithfulness. Isaac was the one through whom the promise of descendants more numerous than the stars would be fulfilled. And Abraham was supposed to sacrifice him? No way. I would have balked. "You can't be serious, Lord. This is my son, my only son."

But the ever faithful Abraham doesn't balk. He says, "Here am I." Holding the boy by the hand, he leads him up the mountain step by grievous step. And when Isaac turns to him and says, "The fire and the wood are here but where is the lamb for the burnt offering?" Abraham says, "God himself will provide the lamb."

He sounds absolutely certain. So much so that centuries later, St. Paul wrote that Abraham's faith was reckoned to him as righteousness.

But surely on that long dark road up Mt. Moriah his faith lost some of its persuasive power. Did he lift his son up on the altar with unwavering trust? No nervous glances toward the thicket? Or did he lift him up with numb resignation?

The honest young preacher said Abraham did it with unwavering trust. And he commended the same to us. All we needed to do was try harder to trust and our doubts would vanish in a puff of smoke.

I told him later that I respected his advice . . . I really did . . . but trying harder to trust didn't work for me. It was like walking on that awful treadmill in the fitness center. You press on for the prize until you're breathless, but at the end of the workout you're still in the gym with all those sweaty people.

Of course, when you're young, you don't *have* to try harder. Faith is easy. You go to Sunday school and accept everything the teachers tell you. At Easter you push fists full of flowers into a chicken wire cross. "Jesus loves me, this I know."

Flannery O'Connor says that this stage of faith is like an electric blanket. You can huddle under its covers . . . safe and warm and confident. But it doesn't take long for children to poke their heads out and start asking questions. "If God is here why can't I see him?" "You mean he's a ghost?!" Doubt begins to slip in between the covers.

I wish it weren't so. I wish I could be as faithful as a child and never doubt that God himself will provide. Unfortunately, a no frequently slips up behind the yes. I don't know why. I guess it's just life . . . life in all its inevitability. Our long years bring with them so many broken dreams. And a fear that's buried so deep it only surfaces now and then in a primitive cry of despair.

"My God, my God, why hast thou forsaken me?"

Martin Luther said, "Oh, this is a hard rebuff, when God shows himself so earnest and so angry, and hides his grace so high and so deep, as those know very well, who feel and suppose in their hearts, that he will not keep what he has promised."[1]

And the reason this rebuff hits us so hard isn't so much our own grievous disappointment, which is enormous, but the loss of faith.

It even happens to the really righteous ones. Saint Teresa, like Abraham, is one of those whose faith was never questioned, but when she died, it was revealed that she actually had doubts. Imagine that. In the midst of the filth and poverty, the disease and death in Calcutta's streets she doubted God's providential care.

A no behind the yes?

I keep thinking about Abraham on Mt. Moriah and Saint Teresa on the streets of Calcutta. I keep thinking about the thousands and thousands of others in the house of despair. It's the dark night of the soul.

And yet . . . I wonder if that's where faith actually begins. At the point where it seems to end. Not the electric blanket kind of faith but the kind that runs deep like a river, that senses the tenderness of God's love in spite of all the evidence to the contrary. "I believe; Lord help my unbelief."[2]

On the way home from church that day, I was pondering how we can be rescued from the dark night when I remembered a story Bishop Bob Atkinson told. He was on one of his episcopal journeys and stopped at a country restaurant in South Carolina. He ordered a hearty breakfast of bacon, eggs, and biscuits. But when the breakfast came, there was a mound of white stuff on the plate.

"What's that?" he said.

The waitress said, "That's grits."

"But I didn't order grits."

"You don't order it. It just comes."

I suppose that's how faith works. It begins with the longing to be seized by God's tenderness. The longing . . . wanting . . . hoping opens the heart to infinite possibilities.

It conditions the soul to receive.

And faith just comes.

CHAPTER 20

A Network of Grace

When you "downsize" to an apartment or retirement home, you have to give away some of your treasures. There isn't room for two tables here and three chairs there. So I've started thinking about what to give away. I'd like for my children to have something precious. Something that adds to the gladness in their eyes.

But what gift would that be? The antique clock in the hall? The hand-stitched quilt? A painting of Sarah swinging her arms out in a song of laughter? It's hard to know.

Last Christmas we gave our son Matt a lightweight tent for backpacking. He opened it and his smile was as thin as a banjo string. "Mom," he said, "You gave me the same tent last year." Now, how was I supposed to remember what I gave him last year? That was a long time ago.

But I understand his disappointment. Our dog gave me a gift. She's a Brittany Spaniel and spends her whole life stalking beasts in the backyard. Last week she got one . . . brought it to the door and dropped it at my feet. A gift. I would have preferred a flower or something, but what I got was a dead critter. I guess it's the thought that counts.

But I don't want my downsizing gifts to be disappointments. I want them to be as wonderful as those *I've* received over a lifetime.

Ribbons, bracelets, scarves, nightgowns with lace around the collar. And taffy! I love taffy. My daughters always bring a box when they come visit. They hide pieces of it all over the house. (There's nothing like finding taffy in your underwear drawer.)

And yet . . . gifts don't always have to be "things." They can be words, stories, memories. They can be blessings . . . on the house you just sold (along with warnings about the pipes upstairs that freeze in cold weather). They can be gestures . . . simple gestures or grand ones.

I keep thinking about the grand one in the movie *Babette's Feast*. In it a young Parisian refugee prepares a French dinner for a group of quarrelsome neighbors. She had been hired to keep the house clean and cook a meal of boiled fish and tea. Every night . . . boiled fish and tea, which the neighbors consumed in hostile silence.

Then, after a few years, Babette inherits some money and asks permission to prepare a French dinner for the group. They agree but they're a bit nervous about a departure from boiled fish and tea. As the appointed day approaches, they worry that they may have placed themselves in the hands of someone who might weave a spell over them.

Indeed, Babette does weave a spell. With *blanquette de veau, pomme de terre, soufflé au fromage*. The group begins to talk to each other. They laugh and their faces are flushed with the joy of good wine. It was a beautiful gift. . . a really beautiful gift.

But lately I've started wondering if I'm *too* focused on giving . . . even though I'm downsizing. Last Sunday in church I received a gift from a child in the next pew. Her mother had given her crayons and a notebook to keep her busy during the sermon. It worked. She scribbled page after page, flipping them over as she made stick people with a purple crayon.

When she saw me watching her, she tore one of the pages out of the book and held it out for me. A gift. I hesitated . . . just for a second . . . but in that second her face showed disappointment. I quickly recovered . . . took the picture and thanked her profusely. But it made me think if perhaps sometimes it's more blessed to *receive* than it is to *give*.

Henri Nouwen, in his *Gracias! A Latin American Journal,* speaks about the way we as missionaries in the north tried to give people in the south what we thought they needed. "But," he said, "we have now come to realize that our very first vocation is to receive their gifts to us and say thanks."[1]

Isn't that also what the gospel tries to tell us? God gave us the grandest gift of all . . . himself. And over a lifetime we've been trying to learn how to *receive* that gift. With songs of praise, discipleship, offerings, bread, wine, love. Mostly love.

So maybe I shouldn't worry so much about *giving* gifts as *receiving* them. To be vulnerable to the other's grace even if it's only stick people. As parents and grandparents we've spent our lives giving, feeding, dressing, teaching, healing. And in an overweening pride we could easily imagine ourselves to be the source of all goodness.

I'm going to forget about the antique clock, the handmade quilt, the painting of Sarah swinging her arms out in a song of laughter. I'm going to sit in the proverbial rocking chair and wait for a child to give me a scribbled page out of her book, a shell from the water's edge, or maybe just a piece of gum.

I'm going to wait for a young man to take my arm and lead me across the street, a young girl to brush my hair and tell me how nice I look. I'm going to wait for God's blessings to fall like blossoms from the vine. And in the reciprocal network of grace in which the giver becomes the receiver and the receiver becomes a giver . . . I'm going to say *gracias*. If only I can remember that I'm not the source of all goodness.

CHAPTER 21

Kingdom Come

I WISH JESUS WERE A LITTLE MORE EXPLICIT. HE NEVER SAYS what the Kingdom of God *is*. He just says what it's *like*. It's *like* a bit of yeast, a treasure in the field, a pearl of great price. It's *like* a mustard seed.

His images always represent something small. Something hidden. If we cover the mustard seed with dirt, it disappears. If we mix a spoonful of yeast with flour and water, it's no longer visible. Same with the treasure and the pearl . . . they're hidden before they're found.

And there's such a huge discrepancy between the humble, insignificant beginnings and their ultimate yield. The mustard seed grows into a tree so tall that birds of the air make nests in its shade. The pearl and treasure are worth more than everything we own. And the woman with the yeast mixes it with three measures of flour. That's a lot of flour! Together with the yeast and water, it yields a huge lump of dough. Not the kind you'd use to bake a few French rolls. But the kind you'd use to bake bundles of bread for a church picnic.

It's amazing. Over the top. But what's it all about?

I used to think it was all about heaven . . . you know, the real one . . . up there. The one we'll discover when "we go to our reward" as my mother used to say (which was probably presumptuous of my mother). Where there will be peace . . . peace that passes all human understanding.

But now that I've prayed the Lord's Prayer a few thousand times, I'm not sure that's what Jesus meant. "Thy Kingdom come; thy will be done on *earth* as it is in heaven." He wasn't talking about a peaceable Kingdom "up there." He was talking about a peaceable Kingdom on *earth*. Which, of course, seems absolutely impossible in our culture of violence and wars within wars. And yet . . . every now and then . . . you can seize a transient moment . . . a miraculous moment when the Kingdom breaks into time.

It was the summer that the inner city of Baltimore burned . . . with protestors on one side of the conflict and a police barricade on the other. Each asserting its righteous claim to be there.

And in the middle of all the violence a young African American boy walked across the street and faced a policeman in riot gear. He stood there for a few minutes and looked up through the man's shield. Then he pulled from his arms a bottle of cool water and gave it to him.

The image went viral, as they say, and thousands . . . maybe hundreds of thousands saw what happened. The seed of human kindness had transcended the desire to dominate the other. And there was the same huge discrepancy between the small boy and the ultimate yield of his gesture . . . a lavish, extravagant, over the top moment of peace.

It made it easy for me to understand why the person who discovered a treasure in the field was willing to sell everything . . . her car, the house, her grandmother's locket . . . everything for a time when the wolf would dwell with the lamb; the leopard would lie down with the kid; the calf and the lion and fatling would live peacefully together; and a little child would lead them.

I suppose I'll never know what the Kingdom of God *is*. In fact, I don't think Jesus even *want*s me to know. I think he wants me to be restless . . . always searching. But at least I know what the Kingdom of God is *like*. It's *like* a bit of yeast, a treasure in the field, a pearl of great price, a mustard seed.

It's *like* a bottle of cool water.

Chapter 22

Big Why Question

My grandson Henry used to ask a lot of questions: "If Jesus had a brother, wouldn't he also be the Son of God?" (Henry, being a twin, is a bit sensitive when it comes to his brother's priority.) I answered his questions as best I could . . . except once. It was years ago on a fall afternoon and Henry came home in a torrent of tears.

"What's the matter, Henry?"

"It's TJ! . . ."

"What happened? . . . Henry! Tell me what happened."

"TJ . . . he was in an accident. At the end of the Farms Road . . . this car came around the corner . . . like really fast . . . and crashed into his father's truck . . . they called the ambulance but it didn't do any good. TJ . . . he died."

I wrapped my arms around his thin shoulders and held him until he could breathe again. Telling him all the while how sorry I was. TJ was a good kid. He raked leaves for everyone in the neighborhood and when it was done, he'd pick up the younger boys and throw them in the piles. They'd come home full of laughter and covered in leaves.

"I'm so sorry, Henry."

His crying slowly eased . . . and then came the question.

"Why did he have to die?"

What can you say? It's one thing to enter a child's grief and try to lift its weight off his heart. But the big why question? It's impossible to answer.

We can knock on the door of the eternal forever . . . just the way Job did . . . and challenge the Almighty to tell us why bad things happen to good people . . . why bad things happen to *young* people. It doesn't seem fair. We queue up according to our age, the hour we were sent into the vineyard. And we're supposed to exit in the same order. The first should be first and the last should be last. So why do the young have to die?

"I don't know, Henry. I just don't know."

I think Henry's grieving would have continued to an eventual place of peace, but someone at school, thinking she was giving good advice, said, "Well, I hate to say it but some people think God punishes us because of our sins. Maybe that happened to TJ."

Henry stood up and yelled, "TJ wasn't a sinner!"

He was sent to the principal's office. (I wish I had been there.)

Weeks passed and the child began to heal. One day he tried to rake the leaves in his yard . . . scattering them into haphazard piles and falling backward into them.

He came over to see me when he heard I had made some mulled cider. I gave him a warm cup and told him I had a story to tell him. It's by a man named Thornton Wilder and it begins on a high road in Lima, Peru. ("Where's that?")

Brother Juniper, an Italian missionary ("What's a missionary?"), sees a famous bridge in the distance. It was a ladder of thin slats swung out over the gorge with handrails made of dried vines. But at that very moment the bridge snapped in two and four people fell down into the gorge. ("Did they die?")

Brother Juniper thought the victims must have been punished because they were sinners. ("That's what that stupid woman at school said about TJ.") But since some folks in the village didn't believe him, he decided to prove his argument. He went out and knocked on all the doors in the neighborhood, asking questions

("Did the neighbors live next door?") to determine how good or how bad the people were. And he rated each person with a number . . . one to ten. ("Was a ten real good?")

Then he drew up a chart on the blackboard . . . putting the scores of those who fell off the bridge in one column and their neighbors in another column. And when he added up the scores, guess what! Those who fell off the bridge were *five* times as good as their neighbors. *Five* times![1] ("That's pretty good.")

"So Henry, you need to remember that story whenever anyone suggests that someone like TJ died because he was a sinner. OK?"

"OK."

"Also . . . remember that Jesus suffered the worst death that anyone could ever suffer . . . hanging on a cross with nails in his hands and feet. And he wasn't bad, was he? (Henry hesitated a little too long for my satisfaction, but a quick poke prompted the right answer.) Will you remember that?"

"Yes."

"And keep on asking questions, Henry. Questions are sometimes better than answers. Especially when you ask questions of God. You may not get an answer right away. But God hears you. He's actually so near you can almost hear him crying because one of his children has died.

"Henry, what did I just tell you?"

"You said God was crying."

"What else was I saying?"

"I don't remember."

"I said to keep on asking questions. And one more thing, Henry. God loves you. Whether you know it, or believe it, or even care about it when you grow up. God loves you. Remember that. OK?"

"OK . . . can I have another cup of cider?"

CHAPTER 23

A Reluctant Prophet

As I was driving through Rockfish Gap the other day I heard the old Beatles song "All You Need Is Love." It was one of those moments when a scene from the past pushes itself into the present and it was the 1960s again. I was stepping over a crowd of college students outside the post office. They were protesting the Vietnam War and an odd sort of fragrance . . . like that of a musk rose . . . drifted over their heads.

A young man in a tie-dyed shirt asked me to join their demonstration, but I told him I had to mail a package. So he moved out of the way and let me pass. "Peace," he said. I said, "Peace" back at him.

But it was an edgy encounter.

From the post office window I could hear them singing, "All You Need Is Love." And being a respectable thirty-year-old, I thought, "Sure! That's all *they* need . . . with parents paying their tuitions and love being so cheap. All you have to do is hug each other and the world will blossom into peace."

I was such a *prig*.

Back in Rockfish Gap I could hear the Beatles long after their voices had vanished from the radio waves. And I thought maybe love *is* all we need. But it's confusing because we use the same word to describe the way we feel about our partners and the way we feel about chocolate macaroons. We love them both.

And yet isn't love . . . in the context of Christian belief . . . something planted like a seed in the soul that finds expression in good works? Back in the 1960s they said we should express it by making love not war. And thousands of young, healthy people decided that was a really good idea.

But I don't think that's what Jesus was talking about when he turned to Peter and said, "Peter, do you love me?"

"Of course, Lord," said Peter. "What a silly question."

But still Jesus asked, "Do you love me?" There was urgency in his voice. "Feed my sheep." Over and over again. "Feed my sheep."

He wasn't talking about a sentimental attachment. He was talking about healing the sick, putting food in outstretched hands, lifting the dispossessed off the streets. And you get the idea that without such concrete acts of love, there was nothing but a word rattling in the wind.

But what was new to me . . . thinking back on that day in the post office . . . was the idea of *confrontation* as a concrete act of love. "Feeding" included protests, demonstrations, sit-ins? I'd grown up in a culture that demanded respect for authority . . . especially the authority of elders. If I was upset I pouted! (Sometimes I refused to speak for thirty minutes.) But I didn't confront. I didn't challenge. And I definitely didn't stage a sit-in outside a United States Post Office. So what was it all about?

The fog around Rockfish Gap began to dissipate in the warmth of the morning. I turned off the highway and drove through long stretches of grassland with weathered barns and split-rail fences. But I couldn't stop thinking about that day in the 1960s. Had its memory bubbled to the surface for a reason?

Does love require *me* to confront? Does it require me to confront the escalation of yet another war as well as the injustice of certain social structures? Henri Nouwen said, "We cannot set the captives free when we do not confront those who carry the keys."[1] Amen to that. And yet today confrontation has dissolved into violence. People on the streets are screaming racial epithets, breaking windows, killing each other. What's happening shames the name of love. "I can't do that, Lord."

I drove on through the valley and tried to think about the day ahead. But the bothersome question kept niggling at my mind. "Do you love me?" Over and over again. "Do you love me?" I knew whose voice it was.

"Yes, Lord, I love you. You are my God, my Holy Friend and it would be wonderful to offer you a fragment of the love that you've offered me over a lifetime. Indeed, I long to do that. I long to be delivered from a polite and indifferent voice. But I'm afraid of violence. If that's the kind of confrontation you're calling me to, maybe you should review my profile. Remember . . . I'm not as young as I used to be."

It was getting late. I crossed over a battered bridge where the waters of John's Creek flattened into the sunlight. The clouds above seemed to be running before the wind. And I remembered the way those students at the post office sat down right in front of the door and protested the war. For all the funny smoke in the air, there was energy in their confrontation and commitment. They were prophets in the wilderness but they didn't scream and break windows. It was a peaceful confrontation.

Like the march from Selma to Montgomery . . . nonviolent in the face of violence. And like the Tank Man in Tiananmen Square. He just stood there . . . like a rock in front of a tank. A nonviolent resistance to Beijing's oppression.

And like Jesus himself! Jesus was a Tank Man! People usually picture him as meek and mild but they forget how he confronted tax collectors, hypocrites, priests, Pharisees. He confronted *prigs*. But he didn't scream or break windows.

"So tell me, Lord. Can I be a Tank Man like you? Can I stand like a rock between violent protests on the one hand and passive indifference on the other? If you think that's possible, I'll answer your call. But remember . . . you'll need to give me a lot more courage than I have now." And one more thing . . .

I'll need more than a Beatles song for blessed assurance.

OK?

CHAPTER 24

A Lot of Unlearning

WHEN I WAS A CHILD WE OFTEN TOOK ROAD TRIPS THROUGH Tennessee and I spent endless hours in the backseat of the car . . . watching billboards float by the window. My favorite one was the red and white flicker for Burma Shave:

The chick he wed,
let out a whoop;
felt his chin,
and flew the coop.

There were signs for Mail Pouch Tobacco and every few miles there was one that said, "See Rock City." (My father never would stop and let me see Rock City.) But the sign that puzzled me the most was one that said JESUS SAVES. And it wasn't just on billboards; it was splashed across the side of barns and on the rooftops. And I wanted to know *what* Jesus saved. Stamps? Coins? Rocks from Rock City?

I asked my mother what it meant and she said not to worry. "Episcopalians don't say that." So I finally concluded that there was no object to the verb. "Save" meant Jesus was just naturally frugal.[1]

I had a lot of unlearning to do.

But I saw the sign again yesterday . . . painted on a wall in bold block letters. JESUS SAVES. And the same question came to mind. What/whom does Jesus save?

The writer of the letter to Timothy said, "Christ Jesus came into the world to save sinners."[2] And we usually think of "sinners" as *really* bad people . . . murderers, adulterers, drunkards, and the like. We can point a finger at them.

But wasn't the writer to Timothy saying that we're *all* sinners?

I keep thinking about that esoteric system of the Enneagram . . . the geometric puzzle with a circle and crazy triangles. According to Enneagram tradition there are nine personality types and *all* of them are subject to temptations . . . hypocrisy, anger, greed, vanity, and so on. It's just a question of which triangle fits your personality. What's your "besetting sin" as they used to say.

Unfortunately, I seem to have nine "besetting sins." So maybe I'm one of those that Jesus needs to SAVE . . . my mother's *savoir faire* notwithstanding.

And yet . . . thanks to the words of a few fiery preachers, I've always considered salvation to be up to me. Sort of like earning a Girl Scout merit badge. "If at first you don't succeed, try, try again." So I work hard at the office, say my prayers, and attend church regularly. I even clean the house . . . occasionally.

But with the coming of age, I've discovered I'm not quite as capable as I used to be. I can't walk up the stairs without a little help from Denny. And getting out of a car? I put the right foot out first, wait a minute to make sure it's found solid ground, then ease out the left one. Not exactly a picture of grace. And as for those besetting sins, I try, try again. But for all my efforts, salvation seems to be in vain. I'm still the same.

Maybe there's a message in my weakness. Maybe it's a good thing to unlearn that sense of self-sufficiency.

I remember C. S. Lewis's classic *The Voyage of the Dawn Treader* about young Eustace who was greedy for the privileges of Narnia. And as a consequence he acquires a dragon's skin . . .

a tough, hard dragon's skin covered with sharp scales. He tries to change his ways . . . but he can't seem to peel away the dragon's skin. Then . . . out of the clouds, slipping between the mountain peaks, Aslan, the great Lion, appears. Clothed in the sun, he descends to the valley, and seeing the boy in such despair, he says, "Here, let me help you." Eustace is willing to let him help. And the Lion scrapes away the sharp scales . . . scrapes and scrapes until finally the boy stands up . . . smooth and soft as a peeled switch.

It's such a beautiful story. Imagine being "smooth and soft as a peeled switch." But isn't C. S. Lewis saying something more? Isn't he inviting us to imagine a time when it's OK to be vulnerable . . . OK to be helpless. Because the Lion (our beloved Lion) will scrape away the sharp scales?

I probably need to act as if I didn't know that . . . or couldn't even *imagine* it. And do what the fiery preachers said. Try, try again. At least the effort would show that, like Eustace, I was willing.

But the truth is . . . JESUS is the One who saves. Not Jane or Julie or Jim or Denny . . . but Jesus. And that's good news.

It should be splashed across the side of barns.

And on the rooftops.

JESUS SAVES.

CHAPTER 25

Ethan

It was Maundy Thursday and the priest did something the congregation had never experienced. He washed our feet. He washed our calloused, bruised, work wearied feet. It was such a humble gesture.

And it was exactly what Jesus did. On the night before he died, he didn't give a sermon or write a book. He got up from the table, laid aside his garments, and tied a towel around his waist. Then he poured water into a basin and began to wash his disciples' feet.

I wonder what he may have said to those whose feet he held in his hands.

"You've walked for miles on these feet, haven't you? I'm sure sometimes you just wanted to sit down and give up."

"Where did you get this scar?"

"Not to worry—feet have memory. They know what it's like to walk on the dark earth."

Then again maybe he didn't say anything. Maybe he knew that for some the impropriety of the gesture was embarrassing. Or the wounds of the heart had settled in their feet and were still too raw for words. So all he did was pour warm water over them and wipe them with a towel. It's such a wonderful story. And such a simple act of kindness. It made me cry. Like an old woman whose face was meant to channel tears.

After our priest put away the basin and towel, he gathered us around the table and shared the last of Lent's bread and wine. Then the Altar Guild stripped the sanctuary of everything . . . candles, cushions, vessels, vases, tapers, linens. Everything was taken away. Only the altar remained.

That night . . . long after the house had gone to sleep . . . I kept wondering why the service had had such a profound effect on me. Then in the half-light of dawn I dreamed it was the Crucified One himself who tied a towel around his waist, poured water into a basin, and washed my feet. I knew he knew that the wounds of my heart were still raw.

Our son had died.

His name was Ethan.

"We always seemed to be looking for him in places after he had gone on. Like children flocking to an Easter egg sighting, we ran to his joy, but he had gone on and we were left looking where only the echo of his generous laughter remained." That's how his brother Matt tried to explain it. Ethan had gone on.

The emptiness of his absence was like that of the sanctuary . . . a vacuum, a nothingness, silence, a space that had been his.

But when I woke up in the morning I remembered how in my dream the Crucified One poured warm water over my feet and told me things that I had always known but never experienced. When he washed his disciples' feet, he was doing something much more than offering a gesture of hospitality. Something much more than trying to remove the dust of city streets. "Unless I do this for you," he said to Peter, "you will have no share of me." In other words, he was once again incorporating himself into the human condition with all its joys, its laughter, its losses.

Jesus would die that day. It would leave an emptiness, a vacuum, nothing, silence, a space that has been his. But in the mystery of the incarnation, he would lift up the wounds that had settled in my feet . . . the ones that he had washed with such tender compassion. He would lift them all the way up to his shoulders and hold them there. Then he would lift them up even higher. And higher.

Over time the vision has started to fade . . .

like a timid ghost that only lingers for a moment.

But feet have memory.

CHAPTER 26

Twilight of Sin

I WAS ENJOYING A QUIET MEAL IN MY MOTHER'S NURSING HOME when she turned to me and said, "Jane, I really like saying that confession about my manifold sins and wickedness, but tell me, Jane," and she moved in a little closer, "what *are* my sins?" And with that she swept her hand over a sea of white headed women and said, "How could anyone sin in a place like this?"[1]

For my mother, sin had to do with sex. And she told me the same thing when I was a teenager. Being good meant you were limited to modest activity in the front seat of the car (which fortunately didn't have a console between the driver's side and the passenger's side). The windows would get all foggy and just about the time things got interesting my father would blink the lights on the front porch. How could anyone sin in a place like that?

But the really *big* sin in those days was disobedience. Which was reinforced every time the preacher told the story of the Fall . . . how the first family was told NOT to eat of the fruit on the tree in the middle of the garden. But they did it anyway. Causing them both to be expelled from their bower of bliss.

And because of all those warnings I stood . . . in Paul's words . . . fairly "blameless before the law." My report cards said, "If she would just settle down." But they never said I was disobedient.

(Which is probably why I was so confused when disobedience suddenly became a virtue. As in *civil* disobedience.)

But as I enter the late afternoon of life, it seems important to answer my mother's question. I've knelt on the hardwood floor for hundreds of successive Sundays and confessed to manifold sins and wickedness as if I felt really bad . . . *mea culpa, mea culpa . . .* when actually I didn't because I didn't know what my sins were.

And it's still hard to know what they are. Sins seem to be whatever the dominant culture says they are. The book of Leviticus lists seventy-six, including carelessly uttering an oath, not standing in the presence of elders, cursing your mother or father (punishable by death), making tattoo marks on your body, and mixing the fabrics in your clothing. The Christian testimony is just as specific.

Paul says . . . in his letter to the Romans, "I do not understand my own actions. For I do not do what I want, but I do the very thing I hate. . . . In fact, it is no longer I that do it but the sin that dwells within me, that is in my flesh."[2] He seemed to be saying that there's a destructive *pattern of behavior* . . . a "sin *(singular)* that dwells within." It can easily tempt you to "do the very thing [you] hate."

Augustine of Hippo called it "original sin." In other words, Adam's fatal nibble was passed down from generation to generation. And the result was "total depravity." That's *total* depravity. Not a pattern of behavior that *tempted* you to do the thing you hate but a predetermined force that *dragged* you into sins.

It's no wonder the word "sin" disappeared from our lexicon. Karl Menninger in his 1973 classic, *Whatever Became of Sin?*, said that Augustine's fatalism was compounded by the threat of dreadful and inescapable consequences. If you sinned you could end up like Hester Prynne in *The Scarlet Letter*, standing on the scaffold with the weight of a thousand eyes fastened on your mark of shame.[3]

Calling something "sinful" became too expensive. So we stopped sinning. We "made mistakes." We "failed." We were sick. We even committed "crimes." But we didn't sin . . . except with a wink and a nod when we ate a piece of chocolate cake.

And even the "mistakes" and "failures," "sickness" and "crimes" were someone else's fault. With the threat of hellfire and damnation our defense mechanism kicked in and we instinctively deflected responsibility to someone else. As Anna Russell says in her "Psychiatric Folksong":

> At three I had a feeling of
> Ambivalence toward my brothers,
> And so it follows naturally
> I poisoned all my lovers.
> But now I'm happy; I have learned
> The lesson this has taught;
> That everything I do that's wrong
> Is someone else's fault.[4]

A lot of what we do *is* someone else's fault. I agree. Mistakes, failures, sickness, and crimes are often determined by environment. Children have been neglected and abused . . . finding their solace in drugs and street gangs. Schools have often failed the most destitute. Poverty has left a skeletal humanity in its wake.

So even though I grew up in a relatively stable environment, I could easily blame the environment. Are my sins really mine?

There's something in me that says yes. Maybe it's a compulsive desire to bring closure to all the things I've done and left undone. To find peace before the sun sets. Whatever. At this stage in life I have to admit that everything I do that's wrong *isn't* someone else's fault.

It's the same story . . . back in the beginning . . . when the Lord God appeared in the garden and asked the man why he had eaten of the forbidden fruit, the man said, "The woman *whom you gave me,* she gave me fruit from the tree, and I ate." Then the Lord God said to the woman, "What is this that you have done?" and the woman said, "The *serpent tricked me* and I ate." ⁵ Someone else's fault? As they say in the country world, "that dog won't hunt."

I never answered my mother's question and I never answered my own . . . at least not adequately. Maybe I can't. Maybe all I can do is keep on confessing to sins known and mostly unknown.

Also . . . should I ask if I am in some way responsible for the sins of others? Do *I* contribute to the mistakes, failures, sickness, and crimes of our culture? It's a radical idea. And my defense mechanism kicks in immediately. *Me?! No way!* But to find peace before the sun sets, maybe I should consider the possibility. As Alexander Solzhenitsyn said in his Nobel Laureate speech, humankind's "sole salvation lies in everyone making everything his business."⁶

CHAPTER 27

Seventy Times Seven

I'm not a reckless driver. In fact, I creep down the road so slowly that there's usually a line of cars stacked up behind my bumper. Some of the drivers make very rude gestures when they pass.

I did get a ticket once in Staunton, Virginia. The officer said I'd gone through a red light (which I distinctly remember being yellow . . . or maybe orange). And what made the arrest so embarrassing was that it happened right in front of my church. I told the officer I was worried that some of the parishioners might have seen me. "Well," he said, "You can tell them you were asking for directions. And here's your ticket."

He had no respect for my collar.

But there was another time when we lived in Connecticut. I was driving up I-95 to see my aunt in Providence, Rhode Island, and I picked up a little speed when I crossed over the state line. Sure enough . . . there was a rotating blue light behind me.

The policeman took my license and registration back to his car. I think he had to check with his dispatcher to see if there were outstanding warrants for my arrest. Finally, he returned, and handed back my documents. Then he said, "It's really dangerous to drive so fast, but if I let you off without a ticket, will you slow down a bit for the rest of your journey?"

"Yes, I promise!"

"Then here's a warning. Speed no more."

I slowed down *a lot*. And with all the windshield time, it occurred to me that I had just been forgiven. In the truest sense of the word. The nice Rhode Island policeman had relieved me of the obligation to pay a traffic ticket.

It was like the parable of the king who held a slave's note for ten thousand talents. But the man, unable to pay the debt, fell down before him and pleaded, "Give me a little more time, please, just a little more, and I will pay you everything." And the king, seeing the man suffer, had compassion on him. "Stand up," he said. And when the man stood before him with the dirt of the ground still printed on his face, the king said, "It's OK. Your debts are forgiven. You are free." He didn't give the man a few months to pay or offer an installment plan with low interest rate. He completely forgave the debt, relieving the slave of the obligation to pay ten thousand talents. That's a lot of forgiveness.

And it was essentially a legal transaction. Just like the transaction between me and the nice Rhode Island policeman. It was based on the decision of one party not to seek compensation from the other party. In other words, not to follow the ancient Mesopotamian law of an eye for an eye, a tooth for a tooth.

But the decision of one party not to seek compensation from the other party isn't easy. The slave in the parable never could reach that point. He was forgiven ten thousand talents, but he couldn't turn around and forgive the one who owed *him* a debt. He wanted an eye for an eye. Too bad. And yet forgiveness is a huge struggle. You can feel the cost in your bones.

I keep thinking about the Amish community in Nickel Mines, Pennsylvania. How they forgave a deranged man who stormed their schoolhouse and shot ten young girls, killing five of them, and then himself. Innocent children, sent to school that morning in pinafores and pleated bonnets, were covered in blood.

And the parents forgave. They attended the killer's funeral . . . wrapped their arms around his mother and consoled his father.

I wonder how long it would take me to forgive him? Years? Forever? It took the Amish community only a few hours. Somehow they seemed to know why Jesus said we should forgive seventy times seven.

But again . . . forgiveness is a huge struggle. Somehow it's hard to let go of the anger . . . the resentment . . . the desire for payback. "He owes me a debt and I'm going to make him pay!"

Some parties can actually *make* the other party pay . . . satisfy the Mesopotamian law. But do we really want to end our days with all that poison in our hearts? I don't want to. Even precious memories would sour. I'd rather end my days in peace . . . with a smile on my lips. But how can I reach that point?

Maybe what I need to do is remember the times that I've *been* forgiven . . . by the nice policemen who didn't give me a ticket . . . by the ones I've neglected, excluded, offended, failed to support in their time of need. And by God himself who often is the only One who knows how thoughtless I was.

That's probably what we all need to do . . . remember.

And then . . . when we realize how many times we've *been* forgiven, it will surely be easier *to* forgive. It may take months . . . even years to reach that point. But once there, and with God's help, we can turn to another and say, "It's OK. I forgive you. You're free."

And . . . in the grace of time we will also be free.

In peace . . . with a smile on our lips.

It's worth a try.

CHAPTER 28

Yielding to Judgment

THE NAME OF THE MOVIE IS *FRIED GREEN TOMATOES*. KATHY Bates . . . or Evelyn as she's called in the movie . . . is driving through a crowded mall looking for a place to park. Finally she sees a man backing out so she waits to take his place. But just as he pulls away, a sassy little red convertible whips into the opening. And two ditzy girls hop out of the car. Evelyn is dismayed. She leans out the window and says to the ditzy girls, "I was waiting for that spot" . . . expecting, perhaps, an apology. But the ditzy driver says, "Yeah? Tough! Face it, lady, we're younger and faster."

There's a long pause in the parking lot, but slowly a secret smile curls up on Evelyn's face. She puts her big fat Chevrolet into gear, presses the accelerator, and rams the sassy little red convertible. She rams it again. And again. Like an avenging warrior . . . yelling "Tawanda!" every time. And when the ditzy girls run out to see what's happening, she says, "Face it, girls. I'm older and I have more insurance."

I don't know why the scene gives me such satisfaction, but it does. I'm tempted to hit the Replay button and watch Evelyn do it again. "Tawanda!!" It's called vengeance.

I thought about *Fried Green Tomatoes* the other day because a neighbor of mine actually suggested that *God* was vengeful. Like he was an old hanging judge who wreaked havoc on those who didn't follow the rules. I told her that if that were the case, I'd have to leave the church and wait for *my* God to return.

Not that my God isn't wrathful. He is. But his wrath isn't like Evelyn's. Or that of the ditzy girls. It isn't a divine temper tantrum bent on retaliation. God's wrath is based on our breaking our covenant with him. It's not about arbitrary rules . . . it's about a relationship. "My people have forgotten me."[1]

I'm one of God's people and I forget often. So I have to stand under some sort of judgment, don't I? We can't keep whistling "There's a Wideness in God's Mercy." And we can't be so presumptuous as to think that nothing much is wrong in the eyes of God. Or that God doesn't *care* what we do.

God *does* care what we do. He cares and he judges between right and wrong.

> What more was there to do for my vineyard
> that I have not done in it?
> When I expected it to yield grapes,
> Why did it yield wild grapes?
>
> Now I will tell you
> What I will do to my vineyard.
> I will remove the hedge,
> And it shall be devoured;
> I will break down its wall,
> And it shall be trampled down.
> I will make it a waste;
> It shall not be pruned or hoed,
> And it shall be overgrown with briers and thorns;
> I will also command the clouds
> That they rain no rain upon it.[2]

Harsh judgment. No wall. No hedge. No rain. Sounds a little bit like the wrath of the old hanging judge. But it's not.

The more I listen to the prophets, the more convinced I am that divine judgment doesn't arise out of a vindictive spirit. No crashing of little red convertibles. It arises out of a heart that beats with melancholy. Out of pain and grief and love. "It was I who taught my people to walk. I took them up in my arms. I led them with cords of human kindness, with bands of love. I was to them like those who lift infants to their cheeks, I bent down to them and fed them."[3]

Walter Brueggemann says those words are among the most remarkable oracles in the entire prophetic literature . . . penetrating deep into the heart of God . . . who not only loves, seeks, pleads, and forgives but lets mercy prevail over judgment. "My heart recoils within me. My compassion grows warm and tender."[4]

God's grief matters.

I heard another wonderful story . . . maybe I read it somewhere. I don't know, but it's about a boy with the habit of stealing comic books. That's all he stole. Just comic books . . . from libraries, drugstores, schools, and friends. Then as soon as he finished reading the one he stole, he would take it back and steal another.

His father knew what he was doing and tried to stop him. But somehow the boy's heart was made of stone. So the father did what he hated to do. He spanked the boy. But he felt so bad about it that he immediately went into the next room and cried.

Years later the boy was talking to his mother . . . reminiscing about his father who had died. He said, "Do you know why I stopped stealing comic books?"

His mother said, "Sure . . . because your father finally spanked you."

"No," the boy said. "I stopped because Daddy cried."

And to think that for years I've thought of judgment as an indictment with no redeeming grace. I still think of it as something to be avoided. Because you have to make restitution. Do something to repair the damage . . . renew the covenant. But isn't God's judgment intended to stop the downward spiral of our relationship. Isn't it . . . in a way . . . cause for celebration. "*For you shall go out in joy, and be led forth in peace.*"[5]

Yes, God's judgment arises out of a heart that beats with melancholy. But it ends with the mountains and hills breaking forth in song.

And all the trees of the field
    clapping their hands.
      Alleluia.

CHAPTER 29

Holding On to the Fish

WE HAD BEEN FISHING THE GREEN RIVER FOR ABOUT AN HOUR when suddenly my line tightened. I had hooked a fish! And not any old fish . . . it was a nineteen inch rainbow trout! Leaping out of the water, running down river, rushing for the weeds. Which made it very difficult to land. I was trying to keep the line tight and reel it in at the same time when I stepped into a gap in the flooring of the boat. And fell overboard.

The guide was frantic. "Feet first," he shouted. "Keep your feet downstream." I knew about the feet first thing, but the rapids were pulling me over the rocks so fast that I couldn't swim to shore. "Let go of the rod!" he shouted. "Let go of the rod!" Now I was fairly certain that I could maneuver my way through that stretch of fast water (which I did), but I wasn't sure I would ever catch another fish like that nineteen inch rainbow trout. So I didn't let go of the rod. I held on to it all the way through the swirling eddies until I came to rest in a quiet pool.

I remembered that misadventure the other day when someone tried to tell me that Jesus's resurrection didn't happen. The disciples just *imagined* they saw him after he died. It was an "experiential reality," an inner feeling in their hearts and minds.

I respect that idea. I really do. There's no question that it was an experiential reality. And it still is. We can feel it every time we wake up to a new beginning in life. But I believe in my heart of hearts that Jesus's resurrection was more than an inner feeling. I think it was a *historical* event. It happened. It was real. The tomb was empty. That's the living core of my faith and without it everything else is futile. So I'm going to hold on to that fish.

Of course, the "fish" in question is subject to a lot of criticism. As N. T. Wright said in his book *Surprised by Hope*, "to believe in the resurrection of Jesus is impossible for those who accept what one writer has called 'current paradigms of reality.'"[1] Meaning science.

But I think there's a subtler, suppler, more ambiguous and living paradigm of reality. Not one that rejects science but one that transcends it and passes into a higher and richer truth. St. John recorded it. "See, I am making all things new. Write this for these words are trustworthy and true."[2] And so I do . . . Jesus was raised from the dead. His resurrection anticipates *our* resurrection. *We* will also be raised from the dead. God will put sinews on our bones and breath in our spirit.

For some of us who are approaching the Great Abyss that paradigm of reality is a critical issue. And others . . . even young scientists . . . can't seem to sustain a *complete* denial of it. Maybe the "what if" lingers in their minds. Or maybe it's emotionally impossible for them to face tomorrow with nothing beyond the window. So they acknowledge the possibility of "after life" with vague references that won't offend modern sensibilities.

I have a friend, Julie, who is also a retired English teacher. She and I are amused by the way the English language gets butchered with misplaced modifiers and dangling participles. She called one day and said, "Jane, pack your bags. Pack your bags. We have to go to Palmyra."

I said, "Why?" (Palmyra is just a junction on the road to Richmond.) But my friend insisted. "Go read the morning obituaries . . . third column halfway down the page." I did as she told me and there was the obvious reason for the urgency of her request.

The obituary read, "Charlie Smith has gone to be with the Lord in Palmyra."

I trust Charlie found a way to be with the Lord before he died . . . in Palmyra or wherever. And I must admit "gone to be with the Lord" is one of those vague references that offers comfort for the bereaved. As do the words of the eulogist who said his friend "had vanished into a thousand winds and the sunlight on ripened grain." That was a good warm Buddhist assurance. As was the Platonic assurance that the soul has escaped the body and floats freely in the halls of heaven.

But again . . . *my* faith is centered on the resurrection. And no matter how many rocks I bump into . . . no matter how many swirling eddies I encounter or how many critics say "Let go of your rod," I believe that Jesus was raised from the dead. He walked the road to Emmaus and cooked fish and sweet potato pancakes for his disciples. (They had caught some really nice fish. A few were nineteen inches.) And he promised that we would *also* be raised from the dead.

I do not know how or when. I do not know if it will be in a life after life after death . . . following one short rest. Or how "embodied" we will be. All I know is that the earthly event of Jesus's resurrection launched a promise for a world surprised by the power of God's miraculous love. And if five hundred years from now scientists proved beyond a shadow of doubt that the dead could never be restored to life . . . and the world could never be made whole again, I would still hold on to that beautiful, glorious, unbelievable truth.

And never let go.

CHAPTER 30

A Fleeting Glimpse

IT HAPPENED WHEN I WAS VISITING MY FRIEND JOHN IN THE hospital. He was drifting in and out of sleep when I came into the room but woke up when he saw me standing at the bedside. We talked, remembered, shared, prayed, held hands. Then I turned to leave. But just as I reached the door, he stopped me. "Jane," he said. "Tell me . . . is it over when it's over?"

I answered with all the assurances of the burial office . . . ones that I'd offered so often to a sea of upturned faces. But suddenly I noticed that the landscape beyond the hospital window was turning gold with the sunset. There was a cemetery on the hillside with hundreds of gravestones. They were standing shoulder to shoulder and the lines engraved across their marble faces made them look as if they were smiling at me.

I don't know what I said to the poor man. I was too taken aback by what I saw. It was a fleeting glimpse of . . . something?

I truly believe that it's not over when it's over. There's a there out there somewhere. Not with a geographical dimension but out there somewhere. And yet it's difficult to explain why I believe that. Most people wouldn't accept an answer that included a bunch of smiling gravestones.

I can usually depend on scripture for help. But scripture is extremely reticent when it comes to life after death. It's much more concerned about life after birth. And when it does mention the possibility, it's elusive, enigmatic. Paul tells the Romans that "if we have been united with Christ in a death like his, we will certainly be united with him in a resurrection like his."[1] That's a blessed assurance, but still . . .

Jesus describes a house with many rooms. I like that possibility. A good Irish priest once said, "You'll have food and raiment, a soft pillow for our head. And may you be forty years in heaven before the devil knows you're dead." I told John that and he smiled.

Then I told him about Dante who sees the approach to *Paradiso* in the resplendent light of his beloved Beatrice's face. And when he finally gets there, it turns out to be a white rose with seats all around . . . sort of like a coliseum.

And folks in *Our Town* imagine fifty miles of elbow room on either side to spare. "I like that better than the coliseum," said John. "I could raise corn that's a mile high."

What else could I offer him? I thought about music. Music can reveal a truth that words can never touch. There's a story told about Handel breaking down in tears after a performance of the *Messiah*. When someone asked him what was wrong, he held up the score and said, "I thought I saw the face of God."

And I told him about *The Shawshank Redemption*, that movie about friendships growing in the context of prison brutality. One day a prisoner who works in the library manages to get into the main office. He locks the door and puts on a piece of classical music, a duet from Mozart's *Marriage of Figaro*. Then he switches all the buttons so the music plays over the loudspeaker into the prison yard. The prisoners stop their work and listen. Music seemed to assure them that there was heaven out there that was free. Totally free.

Then I remembered a dream I had not long after our son died. He was in a blue convertible driving around a boulevard in front of some tall brick houses. I knew it was Ethan because he was wearing his favorite jacket and a tie from Vineyard Vines. So

I packed my suitcase and walked down to the street to wait for him. But he didn't stop. He just drove around the boulevard again and again. Laughing all the way as if he were enjoying the sport of it. Until finally he waved good-bye and drove the straightaway. Out of town.

I couldn't go with him. But I told John that heaven looked like it might actually be fun.

I rambled on and on until I saw that John was falling back to sleep. Bless his heart. He wasn't so much interested in what heaven was like. He just wanted to go there.

I sat in a chair near the window . . . wondering how long it would be. And I thought . . . we just have to wait for our own truth to emerge from the inscape of things . . . from stories, poems, music, dreams, a fleeting glimpse of something.

Before I left the hospital that day I leaned over and whispered in John's ear, "John, it's not over when it's over.

"I know that for sure.

"It's God's truth.

"I've seen the gravestones smile."

CHAPTER 31

Here Hell . . . There Hell

I'M AFRAID OF FIRE. IT HAS A LIFE OF ITS OWN . . . SPREADING ruin in its wake. One spring morning at my father's farm we tried to burn off the back garden. It's what you do to prepare the ground for new growth. We turned the dirt around the edges to contain the fire, but suddenly a gust of wind sent a wisp of burning grass across the road . . . toward my father's barn. We tried to beat it out with our jackets but the fire quickly moved out of control. We could stop the spread in one direction and it would start up in another . . . and another. We won in the end but I'm still afraid of fire.

And every year in the season of Advent, John the Baptist storms through the back door of the church with a fiery message. "The One who is to come will have his winnowing fork in his hand, and he will gather his wheat into the granary; but the chaff he will burn with unquenchable fire."[1] That's unquenchable fire . . . not the kind you can beat out with your jacket. And the Baptist always makes me feel *chaffy* . . . afraid of being consumed with the dried stalks of last year's garden.

Televangelists have used his words to threaten, scold, punish, and frighten . . . suspending people over a pit of fire where they'll fall if they don't mend their ways. *Turn or Burn!* It's really hard for me to imagine going to church and practicing Christian charity because I was *frightened.*

But there's no getting around John the Baptist. His unquenchable fire is a symbol of a future Hell . . . and a very frightening one.

I visited the cathedral in Orvieto, Italy, a few summers ago and saw Luca Signorelli's sixteenth-century painting of the Apocalypse on the walls of the Brizio chapel. It's a fearful picture of Hell with a mass of tormented figures being pushed toward a fiery furnace. "And the smoke of their torment shall burn for centuries and centuries."[2]

In Michelangelo's Last Judgment on the wall of the Sistine Chapel, Charon, the boatman, is beating the damned with an oar as they fall into the corner of glowing coals. The whole artistic testimony of a future Hell is frightening. It can't be real.

I believe there's a Here Hell in the present time. There's ample evidence of that in history . . . Auschwitz, the killing fields of Cambodia, Darfur, Rwanda. In today's paper there's a picture of a dazed five-year-old boy who was pulled from the burning rubble of his home in Syria. There's a lot of Here Hell in the present world . . . inflicted on the innocent.

But a future Hell? I don't know what to say about that. Is there really some place where bad people go when they die? In his book *Love Wins,* Rob Bell considers the possibility. And he figures if there is such a place, it's empty.

Hebrew Scripture refers to a shadowy realm called "Sheol," where people go when they die. But apparently it's not a place of punishment. It's where the just and the unjust alike are housed. Maybe they're even talking to each other.

Jesus refers to "hell" quite often, but the English word is derived from the Hebrew word *Gehenna,* a reference to the city dump southwest of Jerusalem where there's a fire . . . burning constantly to consume the trash.

And remember Shadrach, Meshach, and Abednego? How could anyone forget them? According to the story in Daniel,

Nebuchadnezzar was filled with rage against them and ordered the temperature in the furnace to be jacked up seven times higher than was customary. The strongest guards in his army bound Shadrach, Meshach, and Abednego and threw them into the fiery furnace. But when the King's counselors looked into the flames they saw the men walking around in the middle of the fire. It did not consume them.

I really like those guys.

But still . . . I'm afraid of fire. Even if it does not consume, it threatens eternal punishment, massive torment. And that seems totally inconsistent with God's love.

I wonder if the inconsistency is why the Roman Catholic idea of Purgatory emerged on the theological landscape. Maybe the church *needed* a better place to put their not-so-good families after they died. So out of the compassionate imagination of a thirteenth-century council a halfway house was born. And its purpose wasn't to punish . . . it was to transform.

As Peter Hawkins says in his book *Undiscovered Country,* "Rather than being a penitentiary, in other words, purgatory is a hospital for the healing of brokenness. It is a school for learning the truth . . . a conservatory where soloists become a chorus. Life sentences are not served here so much as lives are rewritten."[3]

It's like the old story about a Desert Father who was responsible for giving spiritual guidance to the young monks in his community. His name was Abbott Joseph.

One day a monk came to see him in despair. He had followed all the rules of his order, done everything right, but he still felt there was something missing in his spiritual life.

"Father," he said to Abbott Joseph. "According as I am able, I keep my little rule and my fast, my prayers, meditation, and contemplative silence; and according as I am able, I strive to cleanse my heart of evil thoughts. Now what more shall I do?" Abbott Joseph rose up in reply and stretched out his hands to the heavens. His fingers became like ten lamps of fire. "Why not be totally changed into fire?"

I guess Abbott Joseph saw fire as something like the one in our spring garden . . . it prepares the ground for new growth.

So even though I don't understand why people believe in a place of eternal torment under the crust of the earth, I can imagine Hell or Purgatory in purely symbolic terms . . . something we suffer as a consequence of wrongdoing. But like Rob Bell, I'm betting on a loving God.

There's a school for learning the truth.

And there's hope of being changed into fire.

CHAPTER 32

Roar of a Lion

NO ONE WANTS TO TALK ABOUT DEATH. THE *D* WORD. THE ONE you only mention when you circle your chairs and can reach out and touch each other. The animal world seems to conspire in making it unmentionable. They go off somewhere and die in the underbrush—behind rocks and leaves . . . so we won't see them.

And yet I remember thinking about the D word when I was just a child. Every night after my bath and a bedtime story, I would kneel by the side of my bed, press my hands into a steeple, and pray:

Now I lay me down to sleep,
I pray the Lord my soul to keep;
If I should die before I wake,
I pray the Lord my soul to take.

When I finished praying, I'd lie under the covers and try to imagine where the Lord would take my soul. Up to heaven where the angels lived? Or under the ground where my grandfather lived . . . in a long shiny box.

Then I grew up and put away childish things. I didn't think about where the Lord would take my soul. I thought about friends in the neighborhood and why I had to go inside and do my homework when it wasn't even dark yet. I thought about the boy who delivered our newspaper. He could ride his bicycle down the sidewalk without holding on.

I thought about where to go to college and about language . . . the grace of words flowing like music off the page. I thought about teaching children who didn't want to study grammar. They just wanted to hear a story. Sometimes it seemed as if their lives were parched for want of deeper water.

Then I thought about a red-headed man who loved Irish literature . . . and took a liking to me as well. We were married on a hot afternoon in June and drove away from home with tin cans tied to the bumper. We settled into an upstairs apartment that cost us $75 a month and were blessed with four children born out of our love for each other. They crawled up in their father's lap to watch cartoons.

Then he died . . . too soon. The D word was no longer an abstraction. It was a reality.

And if you're as old as I am, you frequently think about that reality. The preacher tries to tell you that the deceased isn't really gone . . . he's just slipped into the next room. The preacher means well. He wants to shield us for a brief moment from the sharpness of it all. Sort of like Bottom the Weaver in *A Midsummer Night's Dream*, the player within the play who wants to shield the audience from the roar of the lion. "If I should roar it might frighten the ladies out of their wits, so I will roar as it were a nightingale."[1]

But death doesn't roar as if it were a nightingale. It roars as if it were a lion. It rattles the windows. Stops the clocks. In James Agee's *A Death in the Family*, the young boy says his father "has been dead all night while I was asleep and now it is morning and I am awake but he is still dead and he will stay right on being dead all afternoon and all night and all tomorrow while I am asleep again and wake up again and go to sleep again and he can't come back home again ever any more."[2] Such a sad finality to the child's thoughts.

Mark Twain said he wasn't afraid of dying. He just didn't want to be there when it happened. I'm a little afraid myself. Not of anything specific. It's just the vulnerability of it all that scares me. Being cast loose . . . set adrift in uncertain waters.

But what really bothers me is that I have to die alone. No one will hold my hand, escort me over the threshold, and say, "Watch your step, Jane." And maybe there won't be anyone on the other side to greet me. Maybe it will be like entering JFK airport after a long journey overseas. You search the crowds for a kind-looking man holding up a sign with your name on it. "Ms. Sigloh." And if there isn't a kind-looking man holding up a sign? Do you just walk over to the taxi stand?

Such foolish thoughts.

But the fear of that solitary transition is real. It was the message of one of Martin Luther's most famous sermons: "The summons of death come to us all, and no one can die for another. Everyone must fight his own battle with death by himself alone. We can shout into another's ears, but everyone must himself be prepared for the time of death, for I will not be with you then, nor you with me."[3]

Facing death and facing it alone is probably the biggest challenge to my faith. For most of my life it's been something that happens to *other* people. But now that my time on earth is limited to just a few more years, it's something that could actually happen to *me*. It's out there . . . roaring like a lion.

But in a paradoxical way it reminds me that *life* is also out there. A gift . . . given to me in the beginning. And doesn't faith invite me to respond to the gift by living every moment that's left for me to live?

I'd like to see a new generation born to my children's children, tender of flesh, fat as plums. I'd like to hold them in my

arms, walk down to the river with them . . . show them mayap-
ples with leaves that open like umbrellas in the summer rain.
There's still time left . . .
> to love and laugh and play
> > to dream of tomorrow and
> > > roar as it were a nightingale.

CHAPTER 33

A Good Funeral

AT MY AGE WE GO TO A LOT OF FUNERALS. IT'S WHERE WE *CEL-ebrate* whoever is being buried that week. I went to a funeral yesterday and people said a lot of nice things about the deceased. He was captain of his football team, a member of a fraternity that I forget the name of. And last year he went on a mission trip to Haiti. So, according to the new normal, we celebrated his life.

And yet a lot of us didn't feel that celebratory. A gracious man of God was here. Then he was gone. And we missed him. But the emotional code for a funeral allows a good laugh but not a good cry. It makes you wonder if it's wrong to be sad. When my young husband died, I told my father that I felt like I'd been run over by a Mack truck. He said he didn't want me to say that again.

But is that the way God our Father feels?

Thomas Lynch in his and Thomas Long's book *The Good Funeral* comments on an interview in which a man tells the story of his sister's sudden death. "His mother's grief, her loud weeping, her 'breaking down' was seen . . . as problematic, and she was ushered into a side room behind a curtain where she might be expected to compose herself. As if amplified emotions at the sight of her dead daughter's body in a box were somehow inappropriate.

Like . . . 'breaking down' was caused by some weakness of character."[1] "That's a lie," the man said. "What you need to do is scream,
bang on the wall, tear at your hair, because grief is a primal thing
and the only way out of it is through it."[2]

I don't want anyone to scream at my funeral. (That's all
people would remember about it.) Besides, the death of an old
woman isn't worth a scream. Like Breughel's *Fall of Icarus*, it's
just a splash in the water. But I keep thinking about that passage in Ecclesiastes. "For everything there is a season. A time
to mourn and a time to dance." Shouldn't we give the time to
mourn its due season?

And shouldn't we hold back . . . for just a few minutes . . . the
affirmation of resurrection's promise? Keep it in reserve. Not that
the affirmation isn't important. It's very important. But so is the
bone wrenching reality of death. A good friend was here. Now
he's gone. And before we open the doors to Easter morning can't
we grieve for his absence? Like Rachael who refused to be com-
forted because her children were no more.

William Carlos Williams, in his poem entitled "Tract," gives
advice about the way to give sorrow a proper season.

> I will teach you my townspeople
> how to perform a funeral
> . . .
> you have the ground sense necessary.
>
> See! the hearse leads.
> . . .
> Let it be weathered—like a farm wagon—
> with gilt wheels (this could be
> applied fresh at small expense)
> or no wheels at all:
> a rough dray to drag over the ground.
> . . .

       No wreathes please—
especially no hot house flowers.
Some common memento is better,
something he prized and is known by:
his old clothes—a few books perhaps—
God knows what!

. . .

Then briefly as to yourselves:
Walk behind—as they do in France,
seventh class, or if you ride
Hell take curtains! Go with some show
of inconvenience; sit openly—
to the weather as to grief.

. . .

       Go now
I think you are ready.[3]

I like his advice. And I like the image of a hearse moving from here to there. Slowly . . . "a rough dray to drag over the ground." As Thomas Long suggests, "to accompany the body of that person all the way from here to there is to bear witness to the truth that this was a person of substance and there is a story worth telling about his life."[4] When our good friend Sam Carter died, we went from the "here" of church to the "there" of a graveyard in Ft. Defiance. It was raining but we sat openly to the weather as to grief. And I got the impression that Sam was going somewhere beyond a muddy hole in the ground. He was going to the edge of mystery, the other side of the river, God's country.

And we were accompanying him as far as we could go. Fulfilling that ancient obligation to deal with death by dealing with the dead. Just the way Tobit . . . in the biblical book with his name . . . told his son to do: "My son, when I die, give me a proper burial."[5]

A proper burial meant bathing, anointing, and dressing the body, then taking it to a place of farewell with respect and tenderness.

Also a proper burial says something about the faithfulness of the Church that not only stands beside those who exchange marriage vows and baptize their babies; that not only takes chicken casseroles to the poor and flowers to the sick, but also walks the distance with the ones who have died.

I'm sure my children have the ground sense necessary to walk the distance, but just in case (and with apologies to William Carlos Williams) I'll teach them how to perform *my* funeral.

Here's what you do:
First . . . wash my hands and face.
Don't be afraid of the body!
I'm not going to leap up and say "Boo!!"

Anoint my forehead and straighten my hair
so the bald spot doesn't show.
Then dress me in white . . . an alb, perhaps
the one with lace trimmed sleeves.

Light some candles, and talk to me!!
Tell me how much you'll miss my pancakes.
I'll hear you yet . . . for a while.

Go with me to the funeral home.
Stay there when they press the button
and I go up in flames . . .
enfolded with crimson hands,
like September's rose.

Don't let them put my ashes in a box
that guarantees they will never
be mixed with dirt . . .
I *want* to be mixed with the dirt.
It's from whence I came.

Spend some money on a nice urn
And don't place it on the mantle
next to your father's golf trophy.
Put it on a little table at the front of the church
where the whole congregation can see me.
And maybe mourn . . .

Summon the angels to accompany me to paradise.
And then bury me.
By that I don't mean put the box in the ground
and walk away.
I mean *bury* me.

Put me deep in the ground
where that same day you . . .
with your young arms . . . dug my grave.

No wreaths please . . .
especially no hothouse flowers.
Better to bring me
blossoms from your garden . . .
the wilder the better.
And my old wooden cross
(you know the one I mean).
I want to have it with me.

Take up shovels and toss some dirt in the grave.
Not to worry . . . It'll be like waking up
at night to hear the rain . . .
and going back to sleep again.

Say the blessing.
     Sing the doxology
. . . sing it in gratitude for the life
God gave me in the beginning,
and the life he promised at the ending . . .
Sing it for me.

Then launch some balloons.
Watch them slip free of the earth
and float through bright blue latitudes
to the other side of the river.

Open a bottle of champagne.
Thank everyone for coming.
And pass the deviled eggs.

CHAPTER 34

And Finally

MY HUSBAND LEFT THIS MORNING FOR TWO DAYS OF FISHING. I reminded him of a few things. "Do you have plenty of sunscreen? What about your vitamins? Don't forget your cell phone."

I'm not sure he needed all those reminders, but they go with the territory when you start forgetting things. A friend of mine forgot where she put her glasses. It turns out she'd wrapped them in Saran Wrap and put them in the refrigerator . . . right next to the frozen peas.

Denny's never put his glasses in the refrigerator, but still . . . I need to remind him of things like sunscreen, vitamins, and cell phones. And, bless his heart, he never uses the word "nag" in reference to my advice. (Although he did have a big smile on his face when he pulled out of the driveway this morning.)

In his absence I started thinking about other reminders . . . ones that are bigger than sunscreen. I thought about what I'd tell my children if I didn't think I had much time left to live.

Maybe I'd tell them things like . . . "Never pass up a lemonade stand. Show respect for sand castles. Tend to your brother's grave."

Maybe I'd tell them, "Please teach your children how to write letters. Letters are pieces of paper that you inscribe with words . . . thanking your grandmother for sending you to camp. And when you're finished writing, you fold the paper into a square envelope and put one of those little sticky things in the corner. Then voila . . . it's carried to its destination . . . sometimes in just two days."

Maybe I'd tell them, "Don't forget our homes . . . like the old farmhouse in Springwood. Remember how the floors weren't level and you watched a spill of water roll all the way across the room? You turned it into a game.

"And Mr. Housman's store down the road? Remember? He had a bunch of 'home growns' on the counter . . . yellow squash and tomatoes still warm from the sun. People walked in all day, paid something on their bill, and joked about their neighbors. 'Ain't it the truth?'

"But what was really nice about the store was that in late afternoon, Mr. Housman took down a box of graham crackers and shared them with his customers. I don't know what it was, but that store gave me such a sense of peace."

My children probably won't think graham crackers are such a big deal. But I wish I could go back to Mr. Housman's store.

Maybe I'd ask the children if they remember Stanley, Idaho. "That's where we hiked to the headwaters of the Salmon River. Remember? We fished while chipmunks ate M&Ms from our backpacks. And that night Sally was so tired she fell asleep with her face in the supper plate. We laughed a lot that day, didn't we?"

And I should definitely tell them not to forget the story of their grandfather's parrot. "I told you about it when you were little. The parrot was trained to wake up your grandfather in the morning and one night it started squawking. 'Get up, Tom. Get up, Tom.' The house was on fire and but for the parrot, your grandfather would have died. The parrot *did* die. I don't remember its name but you can call it 'Guardian' or 'Gardie' for short. Gardie was the family martyr so pass the story on to *your* children."

What else?

I should remind them that all the answers aren't in the back of the book.

And that faith isn't static. It's open to new seasons.

"And as for traditions? Some of them are good . . . like writing letters, taking off your cap when you come inside, sitting at the table for dinner instead of picking up a Bubba Burger on the way home."

As Tevye said in *Fiddler on the Roof,* "It's tradition."

"But you should also remember that Jesus frequently disregarded traditions . . . by healing lepers, breaking fasts, ignoring the Sabbath, allowing women to touch the hem of his robe. So you shouldn't feel all that bad if you deposit a few of our traditions in the neighbor's yard sale. Someone will buy them."

What else?

"Remember to take time out from your busy lives to listen for the whisper of a hummingbird's wings. And when summer is full of grace, reach up and pull a ripe peach off a branch. It'll taste good to you.

"So will chocolate ice cream.

"And don't forget that sometimes it's good to be alone . . . Go for a walk in the woods and notice how the skeletal trees of winter start to bloom again."

If I didn't think I had much time left to live I'd probably keep on talking . . . telling them not to forget . . . not to forget. But I know that if I dragged it out too long, they'd start thumbing their cell phones under the table. So I think I'll just say, "Go now and peace be with you."

"No! Wait a minute! I need to remind you of one more thing. Don't forget that . . . sadly . . . there's anguish in every life . . . in *every* life. But it's often in that place of anguish that we learn the meaning of love. John Welch once said, 'With my tears I would water roses, to feel the pain of their thorns, and the red kiss of their petals.'

"Beautiful, right? Don't forget it.

"And don't forget that life must someday end. Mine and yours. Everything goes back to the earth. But I'm as sure as I can be that there is another dimension, something beyond . . . like a field with grasses bending to the wind. It's a field that's just as beautiful as a church on Easter morning . . . and just as sacred.

"So, when *your* days are done, look for me in that field. I may be gathering flowers from the hillside or I may be asleep in the warmth of the afternoon sun. But I'll be there. The gate is open and I'll wait for you.

"Go now. And peace be with you."

Questions for Reflection and Discussion

Chapter 1: Sand Castles

Have any of your long-held convictions shifted in recent years? Are there some that you are protecting with walls and moats?

Think back to a conviction that has changed over the years. How did you feel about its changing? How do you feel about it now?

Chapter 2: Where the Wind Blows

What unknowns trouble you the most?

Look back to what has worried you in the past. Do you have the same worries today?

How would you try to cultivate gracious uncertainty? Does using plastic bags help? If not, what does?

Chapter 3: Hearing and Listening

A standard exercise to determine whether you are hearing and listening is to repeat the person's words and ask if what you said is what he or she said. Try it with a friend.

It's hard enough to hear the words others say, but even harder to understand what may be behind the words. Do gestures and facial expressions match the words? Ask about the feelings behind the words.

One of the worst betrayals is for someone we love not to listen to us. Can you think of a time when someone has not listened to you or not believed you? What was your response?

Chapter 4: Yoke of Freedom

Can you think of a time when you have found rest for your soul by assuming a yoke? When sacrifice has been more fulfilling than freedom?

Someone wrote that happiness is a by-product. A by-product of what?

The author writes that it is paradoxical "that God liberates us . . . and simultaneously binds us to him." From *what* does God liberate us? How is his bondage freedom?

Chapter 5: The Wonder of It All

e e cummings says of the Good Samaritan that he "staggered banged with terror through a million billion trillion stars." Is terror related to wonder?

Science seeks to know *how* the world was made; Religion seeks to know *why*. Do you find that a helpful distinction? Why or why not?

Think of times when you have known something without rational analysis. A feeling, a dream, a prediction. Is it any less real because it is not the product of reason?

Chapter 6: Matter Matters

Baptism is a sacrament, "an outward and visible sign of inward and spiritual grace." What does this definition mean to you? How does God reveal himself to you through tangible things?

What to you is the most significant part of the baptismal service? Why?

CHAPTER 7: EXPECTED SURPRISE

Do you find not only the Christmas traditions but other rituals that suffer from overfamiliarity? Do they breed a certain complacency in your faith?

Can you think of times in your life when someone revealed God to you? Have there been times when you may have revealed God to others?

CHAPTER 8: WHAT'S IN A NAME?

How has your name influenced your life? Why did your parents choose it? How do you feel about it?

If you are angry with someone, does it help to consider that their name is Beloved, too?

To whom do you pray—Abba? Heavenly Father? Dear God? Does how you address God make a difference?

CHAPTER 9: A FENCE IN THE RAIN

"One man loved the pilgrim soul in you," says Yeats. What's a pilgrim soul? What is significant about the fact that this same man in the poem "Loved the sorrows of your changing face"?

Do you think old love is different from young love? Is it better? Explain.

CHAPTER 10: THE WISDOM OF CLAY

Explain the title. Would "Carrying Jesus's Sandals" be a better title? Why or why not?

Was Jesus testing the Syrophoenician woman? Or did he learn something from her about his mission?

Are we worthy to gather up the crumbs under the table?

CHAPTER 11: SEMANTIC SLIPPAGE

Can someone flunk out of confirmation class? If so, how?

If you make a vow, a commitment, a promise, does that mean you must not entertain doubts?

What for you is the difference between believing "in" God and believing statements "about" God (that He is all-powerful, all-knowing, all-loving, for instance)?

CHAPTER 12: TO CLAP OR NOT TO CLAP?

Why do you pray? How do you pray? When do you pray?

If prayer is like conversation with God, shouldn't it include listening? How do you let God speak? What if His language is silence?

What does prayer do for you?

CHAPTER 13: RINGING THEM HOME

Do you have childhood memories of church, either positive or negative, that still affect you? What are they?

If you attend church services regularly, why? If you do not, why not?

What do you first think when you hear the word "evangelist"? Does it have any negative connotations for you? Why? If you think of the word as meaning a bringer of good news, then how do you define "good news"?

CHAPTER 14: LETTUCE IN THE LAP

Think of a time when you have had to acknowledge the limits of your self-sufficiency. How did you feel? What were the results?

The psalmists "voiced their complaints with as much candor as they voiced their praise." Do we? If not, why not? Are we afraid of being impolite or whiny?

CHAPTER 15: TOO DEEP FOR WORDS

Have you heard funny distortions of familiar prayers or words from the Bible?

Think of the times and places where you feel God's presence most strongly. What characteristics do these times and places have? Is silence part of it?

CHAPTER 16: WHY THE CROSS?

How would you explain Christ's death and resurrection to a six-year-old? How do you explain them to someone your age, or indeed to yourself?

Is the question "Why the cross?" the same as "Why is there suffering?" Does the cross suggest that God participates in our suffering? What difference would that make?

In your life, have there been times of the cross that turned into resurrection? Or did not?

CHAPTER 17: THE BIBLE TELLS ME SO

Someone once wrote that the more you learn about almost any activity, the more you enjoy it and profit from it. Learning more about the Bible or Shakespeare or how to swing a golf club can become tedious, but if we persevere, we are rewarded for our endurance. Can you think of examples of the truth of this? Can you think of exceptions?

Someone equally anonymous once wrote that what we love, we want to learn about. Is that true in your experience?

Reread a story from the Bible that you remember from your childhood—Adam and Eve, perhaps, or David and Goliath, or the Birth of Jesus. How has your understanding of the story changed?

CHAPTER 18: WELLSPRING OF GRATITUDE
In *The Life-Changing Magic of Tidying Up*, Marie Kondo argues that most of us have too much stuff, stuff that prevents us from appreciating what we have. Inventory some part of your house—a closet, a dresser, a chest—to see what you no longer have use for, what you had forgotten all about, what might be of use to someone else. See if you discover appreciation for something long forgotten.

CHAPTER 19: YES BEHIND THE NO
In your experience is the author right in saying "trying harder to trust" doesn't work? Consider various kinds of trust—in God, in friends and family, in institutions.

If Abraham had said no to God's command to sacrifice his son, Isaac would have lived. But in the story he lives anyway. What is the difference?

Make a timeline of your faith journey. Pay special attention to those times you felt your faith threatened. When did you feel your faith strengthened?

CHAPTER 20: A NETWORK OF GRACE
Can you think of a gift you have received in the last twenty-four hours? In the last week?

It may be helpful to review presents you have given and presents you have received over the years. Which stand out in your mind as particularly wonderful and which as particularly inappropriate? If someone gave you a gift that you didn't appreciate, did you like that person any less?

When we were children, we often gave pledges to our parents as Christmas presents: I promise to feed the dog all week without complaining. I promise to make up my bed each morning. I promise I will not beat up my brother. As adults, what pledges might we make to our family and friends?

CHAPTER 21: KINGDOM COME

Do you have any other images for the kingdom of heaven? Explain.

Do you *look* for the kingdom of heaven? If so, where? Where don't you look?

A little boy in a riot-torn city gives a policeman a bottle of water. Is the author right to see that as revealing the kingdom of heaven? If so, what does that say about our role in the kingdom? Is it more than looking for it?

CHAPTER 22: BIG WHY QUESTION

Have you had the experience of explaining death to a child? What did you say? Were you satisfied with your answer? Was the child satisfied?

Though the author offers her grandson an explanation, what he remembers is only "God was crying." Do you think her grandson understands enough?

The author tells her grandson finally, "God loves you" and "Keep on asking questions." Would you add anything to her advice? Or is it enough?

CHAPTER 23: A RELUCTANT PROPHET

Have you had the experience of wanting to speak out against injustice (or other wrongs) but did not want to "confront" other people? What did you do?

Are you using the whole range of gifts that God has given you? If the answer is no, then what gifts are you not using?

What do you do to "feed the sheep"? What more could you do?

CHAPTER 24: A LOT OF UNLEARNING

We usually think of maturing in faith as "learning," but the author suggests that we need to "unlearn" as well. In your own faith, what have you needed to "unlearn"?

Think back to the last few days: whom have you lifted up? How? Who has lifted you up? How?

Think of an image that conveys "Jesus saves."

CHAPTER 25: ETHAN

Some things lie too deep for discussion.

CHAPTER 26: TWILIGHT OF SIN

What does sin mean to you? In church tradition, the "deadly" sins are pride, greed, lust, envy, gluttony, wrath, and sloth. Do you find these categories helpful?

Someone once said that the "best" sin is self-righteousness because it is the only sin that does not result in feelings of guilt. Do you agree?

Imagine your life without sin. How would it be different? How would you be different?

CHAPTER 27: SEVENTY TIMES SEVEN

Think of someone you would like to forgive, some resentment you would like to shed. Now imagine why that person may have hurt you. What might have been going on in their life? Could their hurt have caused them to hurt you? Can you break the chain? If so, how?

Why does God forgive us? Could it be because He loves us? Can we forgive without loving?

CHAPTER 28: YIELDING TO JUDGMENT

The Bible tells us to "Judge not lest ye be judged." But there is the judgment of the hanging judge and the judgment of the loving parent. Is judgment done in love permissible?

Think back to some misbehavior of your youth. What caused you to reform?

Imagine yourself a classroom teacher, with one student who is continually disruptive. What measures might you take to get the student to change?

Can you think of a time when the worst consequence of misbehavior was hurting someone you loved?

CHAPTER 29: HOLDING ON TO THE FISH

Though this book is entitled *Gracious Uncertainty*, the author's belief in the Resurrection as a historical fact could be called a "gracious certainty." Does this certainty on her part affect your reading of the rest of the book? How?

Does the story about catching the fish help you understand the author's faith in the Resurrection? Does it help you sympathize with it?

What aspects of your faith demand "gracious certainty" on your part?

CHAPTER 30: A FLEETING GLIMPSE

What is your concept of heaven?

The author describes "fleeting glimpses" of heaven: in dreams, in flashes of beauty. Have you had such experiences? What do they suggest to you about heaven?

If you could design a heaven, what would it look like, feel like, sound like, smell like?

CHAPTER 31: HERE HELL ... THERE HELL

The author describes several depictions in Western art of souls in hell, but in the previous chapter heaven was depicted as a fleeting glimpse. Is it easier to imagine hell than heaven? Why?

Would a loving God create hell?

In our own experience, often something that seems hellacious is transformative. Think of an example.

CHAPTER 32: ROAR OF A LION

Martin Luther writes, "Everyone must himself be prepared for the time of death." How are we supposed to prepare? Can we prepare?

Is it difficult for you to think about the death of friends and relatives? Is it more difficult to think about your own death? Why?

Some argue that recognizing that life will end makes living more intense, even enjoyable. Do you agree?

CHAPTER 33: A GOOD FUNERAL

Have you attended what you found to be a "good" funeral? What about a "bad" funeral? What were some of the differences?

Consider funerals of other religious traditions and other cultures. Have you seen any differences in the way people handle death?

Plan your own funeral. Consider how you hope your friends and family will respond. What do you want your funeral to say?

CHAPTER 34: AND FINALLY

Looking back over your life, are there memories you would not want to be lost when you die? Begin to write them down.

If you could give three pieces of advice to a young person you love, what would they be?

Share the three most important things you have learned over your lifetime.

Notes

Chapter 1: Sand Castles
1. Jeremiah 1:10.

Chapter 2: Where the Wind Blows
1. Job 38:4, 10–11.
2. John 3:8.

Chapter 3: Hearing and Listening
1. Acts 2:1–4.
2. Acts 2:8.
3. Huston Smith with Phil Cousineau, from "Encounters" in *Parabola* 65 (Fall 2012). Excerpted and printed with permission from *And Live Rejoicing* by Huston Smith and Phil Cousineau (Novato, CA: New World Library, 2012).

Chapter 4: Yoke of Freedom
1. Peter Gomes, *The Good Life* (New York: HarperCollins, 2002), 165.
2. Gomes, *The Good Life*, 165.
3. Galatians 5:4.
4. Matthew 11:29–30.

Chapter 5: The Wonder of It All
1. Lawrence M. Krauss, "A Universe Without Purpose," *Huffington Post*, April 26, 2012.
2. Karen Armstrong, *The Case for God* (New York: Alfred A. Knopf, 2009), 9.
3. Psalm 104:1–3.

Chapter 6: Matter Matters
1. Galatians 2:20.

CHAPTER 7: EXPECTED SURPRISE
1. Luke 2:15.
2. *Poems and Prose of Gerard Manley Hopkins*, selected with an introduction by W. H. Gardner (Harmondsworth, Middlesex, England: Penguin Books, 1933).

CHAPTER 8: WHAT'S IN A NAME?
1. Gregory Boyle, *Tattoos on the Heart* (New York: Free Press, 2010), 54.
2. Exodus 33:17.
3. Luke 10:20.
4. Matthew 3:17.
5. Exodus 3:13–14.

CHAPTER 9: A FENCE IN THE RAIN
1. Suzanne Guthrie, "First Love," *Christian Century*, December 16, 1992.
2. Song of Solomon 4: 10–11.
3. William Butler Yeats, "When You Are Old," in *The Collected Poems of W.B. Yeats* (New York: The Macmillan Co., 1933), 40.

CHAPTER 10: THE WISDOM OF CLAY
1. Matthew 3:11.
2. Mark 7:26.
3. Rob Bell, *Velvet Elvis* (Grand Rapids, MI: Zondervan, 2005), 33.

CHAPTER 11: SEMANTIC SLIPPAGE
1. Marcus Borg, *Speaking Christian* (New York: HarperCollins, 2011), 118–19.

CHAPTER 12: TO CLAP OR NOT TO CLAP?
1. Mark Twain, *The Adventures of Huckleberry Finn* (New York: Harper & Bros, 1896), 23.
2. Karen Armstrong, *The Case for God* (New York: Alfred Knopf, 2009), 278.

CHAPTER 14: LETTUCE IN THE LAP
1. Matthew 11:28.
2. Eugene H. Peterson, *The Message: The New Testament, Psalms and Proverbs* (Colorado Springs, CO: NavPress, 1993), Psalm 88.

CHAPTER 15: TOO DEEP FOR WORDS
1. Rumi, "Moses and the Shepherd," translated by Coleman Barks, *The Counselor Magazine*, September 2012.

CHAPTER 16: WHY THE CROSS?

1. "Rock of Ages," *Prayer Book and Hymnal,* according to the use of the Episcopal Church (New York: The Church Pension Fund, 1986), Hymn 685.
2. *The Book of Common Prayer* (New York: Church Publishing, 1979), 334.
3. Alister E. McGrath, *The Mystery of the Cross* (Grand Rapids, MI: Zondervan, 1988), 123.
4. Isaiah 42:6, 43:2.

CHAPTER 17: THE BIBLE TELLS ME SO

1. I Corinthians 2:3.
2. Peter J. Gomes, *The Good Book* (New York: Avon Books, 1996), 13.
3. Gomes, *The Good Book,* 8.
4. Hebrews 4:12.
5. Luke 7:39.

CHAPTER 18: WELLSPRING OF GRATITUDE

1. Mark 12:43–44.
2. 1 Kings 17:12.

CHAPTER 19: YES BEHIND THE NO

1. Rev. E. Mueller, comp., *Luther's Explanatory Notes on the Gospels,* trans. Rev. P. Anstadt, D.D. (York, PA: P. Anstadt & Sons, 1899).
2. Mark 9:24.

CHAPTER 20: A NETWORK OF GRACE

1. Henri Nouwen, *Gracias! A Latin American Journal* (Maryknoll, NY: Orbis Books, 1983), 188.

CHAPTER 22: BIG WHY QUESTION

1. Thornton Wilder, *The Bridge of San Luis Rey* (New York: HarperCollins, 1927).

CHAPTER 23: A RELUCTANT PROPHET

1. Henri Nouwen, *Compassion* (New York: Doubleday, 1983), 124.

CHAPTER 24: A LOT OF UNLEARNING

1. I shared a shorter version of this story in my previous book, *Like Trees Walking: In the Second Half of Life.*
2. 1 Timothy 1:15.

CHAPTER 26: TWILIGHT OF SIN

1. A version of this story appeared in *Like Trees Walking: In the Second Half of Life.*
2. Romans 7:15–17.
3. Karl Menninger, *Whatever Became of Sin?* (New York: Hawthorn Books, 1973).
4. Anna Russell, "Psychiatric Folksong," in *The Crisis in Psychiatry and Religion* by O. Hobart Mowrer (Princeton, NJ: Van Nostrand, 1961), 41.
5. Genesis 3:13.
6. As quoted in Menninger, *Whatever Became of Sin*, 231.

CHAPTER 28: YIELDING TO JUDGMENT

1. Jeremiah 2:32.
2. Isaiah 5:4–6.
3. Hosea 11:3–4.
4. Hosea 11:8.
5. Isaiah 55:12.

CHAPTER 29: HOLDING ON TO THE FISH

1. N. T. Wright, *Surprised by Hope: Rethinking Heaven, the Resurrection, and the Mission of the Church* (New York: HarperCollins, 2008), 69.
2. Revelation 21:5.

CHAPTER 30: A FLEETING GLIMPSE

1. Romans 6:5.

CHAPTER 31: HERE HELL . . . THERE HELL

1. Matthew 3:12.
2. Revelation 14:11.
3. Peter Hawkins, *Undiscovered Country* (New York: Seabury Books, 2009), 52–53.

CHAPTER 32: ROAR OF A LION

1. William Shakespeare, *A Midsummer Night's Dream*, act 1, scene 2, line 84.
2. James Agee, *A Death in the Family* (New York: McDowell, Obolensky 1956), 263–64.
3. Martin Luther, *Luther's Works*, ed. Jaroslav Pelikan and Helmut Lehmann, vol. 51, sermon 1 (Philadelphia, PA: Muhlenberg, 1959), 70.

CHAPTER 33: A GOOD FUNERAL

1. Thomas G. Long and Thomas Lynch, *The Good Funeral* (Louisville, KY: Westminster John Knox Press, 2013), 67.
2. Long and Lynch, *The Good Funeral*.
3. William Carlos Williams, excerpts from "Tract," in *The Collected Poems: Volume I, 1909–1939* (New York: New Directions Books, 1938), 12–14.
4. Long and Lynch, *The Good Funeral*, 214.
5. Tobit 4:3.

Bibliography

Agee, James. *A Death in the Family*. New York: McDowell, Obolensky, 1956.

Armstrong, Karen. *The Case for God*. New York: Knopf, 2009.

Bass, Diana Butler. *Christianity for the Rest of Us: How the Neighborhood Church Is Transforming the Faith*. New York: HarperCollins, 2006.

Bell, Rob. *Love Wins: A Book about Heaven, Hell, and the Fate of Every Person Who Ever Lived*. New York: Harper One, 2011.

———. *Velvet Elvis: Repainting the Christian Faith*. Grand Rapids, MI: Zondervan, 2005.

Borg, Marcus J. *Speaking Christian: Why Christian Words Have Lost Their Meaning and Power—And How They Can Be Restored*. New York: HarperCollins, 2011.

Borg, Marcus J., and N. T. Wright. *The Meaning of Jesus: Two Visions*. New York: HarperCollins, 2007.

Boyle, Gregory. *Tattoos on the Heart: The Power of Boundless Compassion*. New York: Free Press, 2010.

Buber, Martin. *I and Thou*. Translated by Walter Kaufmann. New York: Simon and Schuster, 1970.

Burt, Donald X. *But When You Are Older: Reflections on Coming to Age*. Collegeville, MN: Liturgical Press, 1992.

Chardin, Pierre Teilhard. *The Divine Milieu*. New York: Harper and Row, 1968.

Collins, Billy. "The Afterlife." In *Questions about Angels*. Pittsburgh: University of Pittsburgh Press, 1991.

Finlan, Stephen. *Problems with Atonement: The Origins of, and Controversy about, the Atonement Doctrine*. Collegeville, MN: Liturgical Press, 2005.

Goff, Jacques Le. *The Birth of Purgatory*. Translated by Arthur Goldhammer. Chicago: University of Chicago Press, 1981.

Gomes, Peter J. *The Good Book: Reading the Bible with Mind and Heart*. New York: Avon Books, 1996.

———. *The Good Life: Truths That Last in Times of Need*. New York: HarperCollins, 2002.

Gomes, Peter J., and Henry L. Gates. *Sermons: Biblical Wisdom for Daily Living*. New York: Random House, 1998.

Guthrie, Suzanne. "First Love." *The Christian Century* 109, no. 37 (1992).

Hawkins, Peter S. "Famous Last Words." In *Heaven,* edited by Roger Ferlo, 36. New York: Seabury Books, 2007.

———. *Undiscovered Country: Imagining the World to Come.* New York: Seabury Books, 2009.

Hengel, Martin. *The Atonement: The Origins of the Doctrine in the New Testament.* Translated by John Bowden. Philadelphia: Fortress Press, 1981.

Heschel, Abraham Joshua. *I Asked for Wonder: A Spiritual Anthology.* Edited by Samuel H. Dresner. New York: Crossroad, 2012.

Keck, Leander E. *The Church Confident: Christianity Can Repent But It Must Not Whimper.* Nashville, TN: Abingdon Press, 1993.

Laird, Martin. *Into the Silent Land: A Guide to the Christian Practice of Contemplation.* New York: Oxford University Press, 2006.

Leech, Kenneth. *Experiencing God: Theology as Spirituality.* New York: Harper and Row, 1985.

Lewis, C. S. *The Four Loves.* New York: Harcourt, Brace, 1960.

———. *The Great Divorce.* New York: HarperCollins, 1973.

———. *The Screwtape Letters.* New York: Macmillan, 1982.

Long, Thomas G., and Thomas Lynch. *The Good Funeral: Death, Grief, and the Community of Care.* Louisville, KY: Westminster John Knox Press, 2013.

Marty, Martin E. *Pushing the Faith: Proselytism and Civility in a Pluralistic World.* Edited by Frederick E. Greenspahn. New York: Crossroads Publishing, 1988.

McGehee, J. Pittman. *Paradox of Love.* Houston: Bright Sky Press, 2011.

McGehee, J. Pittman, and Damon J. Thomas. *Invisible Church: Finding Spirituality Where You Are (Psychology, Religion, and Spirituality).* Westport, CT: Praeger Publishers, 2009.

McGrath, Alister E. *The Mystery of the Cross.* Grand Rapids, MI: Zondervan, 1988.

———. *The Unknown God: Searching for Spiritual Fulfilment.* Grand Rapids, MI: Eerdmans Pub., 1999.

McLaren, Brian D. *A Generous Orthodoxy.* Grand Rapids, MI: Zondervan, 2004.

McNamara, William. *Earthy Mysticism: Contemplation and the Life of Passionate Presence.* New York: Crossroad, 1983.

McNeill, Donald P., Douglas A. Morrison, and Henri J. M. Nouwen. *Compassion: A Reflection on the Christian Life.* New York: Doubleday, 1982.

Menninger, Karl. *Whatever Became of Sin?* New York: Hawthorn Books, 1973.

Merton, Thomas. *New Seeds of Contemplation.* New York: New Directions Book, 1961.

———. *Through the Year with Thomas Merton: Daily Meditations from His Writings.* Edited by Thomas P. McDonnell. Garden City, NY: Doubleday, 1985.

Milosz, Czeslaw. *Selected Poems and Last Poems: 1931–2004*. New York: HarperCollins, 2006.

Moore, Peter C. *Disarming the Secular Gods: How to Talk So Skeptics Will Listen*. Downers Grove, IL: InterVarsity Press, 1989.

Nouwen, Henri J. M. *Reaching Out: The Three Movements of the Spiritual Life*. New York: Doubleday, 1975.

Nouwen, Henri J. M., and Walter J. Gaffney. *Aging: The Fulfillment of Life*. Garden City, NY: Doubleday, 1974.

O'Donohue, John. *Eternal Echoes: Celtic Reflections on Our Yearning to Belong*. New York: Perennial, 2000.

Oliver, Mary. *Thirst: Poems*. Boston: Beacon Press, 2016.

Ortberg, John. *Faith & Doubt*. Grand Rapids, MI: Zondervan, 2008.

Pannenberg, Wolfhart. *Christian Spirituality*. Philadelphia: Westminster Press, 1983.

Pelikan, Jaroslav. *Jesus through the Centuries: His Place in the History of Culture*. New Haven: Yale University Press, 1985.

Peterson, Eugene H. *The Message: The New Testament, Psalms and Proverbs*. Colorado Springs, CO: NavPress, 1993.

Robinson, Marilynne. *Gilead: A Novel*. New York: Farrar, Straus and Giroux, 2004.

Smith, Martin L. *Nativities and Passions: Words for Transformation*. Cambridge, MA: Cowley Publications, 1995.

Steindl-Rast, David. *Gratefulness, the Heart of Prayer: An Approach to Life in Fullness*. New York: Paulist Press, 1984.

Sweeney, Jon M. *Inventing Hell: Dante, the Bible and Eternal Torment*. New York: Jericho Books, 2014.

Williams, William Carlos. *The Collected Poems: Volume I, 1909–1939*. New York: New Directions Books, 1938.

Wright, N. T. *Surprised by Hope: Rethinking Heaven, the Resurrection, and the Mission of the Church*. New York: HarperCollins, 2008.

Yeats, William Butler. "When You Are Old." In *The Collected Poems of W.B. Yeats*. New York: The Macmillan Co., 1933.